The Fighting Rifle Book 2

The Fighting Rifle, Volume 2

Mike Harland

Published by Mike Harland, 2021.

THE FIGHTING RIFLE BOOK 2

First edition. November 19, 2021.

Copyright © 2021 Mike Harland.

ISBN: 979-8224269914

Written by Mike Harland.

Also by Mike Harland

Personal Security Detail Operations
Personal Security Detail Operations Book 1
Personal Security Detail Operations Book 2
Personal Security Detail Operations Book 3
Personal Security Detail Operations Book 4

The Fighting Rifle
The Fighting Rifle book 1
The Fighting Rifle Book 2
The Fighting Rifle Book 3

Standalone
Personal Protection And Body Guarding Manual

The Fighting Rifle

Book 2

Basic to Advanced Manual

(The Fighting Rifle)

Dedication

To my family who have always been supportive
of all my endeavors

And all those who serve righteousness with
love and perseverance

About The Author

I was trained for 16-17 years in Karate, reaching black belt 2nd Dan in 1991. During this period, I participated in a number of karate competitions, winning gold and a number of bronze medals in competition. From 1985-1986 did my national service in the South African Defense Force (SADF), doing border duty for 9 months in the combat area (red zone/war zone). As a 20-year-old I saw my first contact (real life shooting) as a group of ANC/ SWAPO terrorist organizations attacked our base. Although it was probably SWAPO as the ANC's "Spear of the nation" army was a bit blunt and lost every contact with SA forces.

From about 1987 till the early 90's I worked doing door duty at clubs. During this period in our country, badly behaved people normally took their punishment like a man, and that was where I had most of my street experience situations up until about 40 years of age. Personally, and in the capacity of a soldier and Close Protection Specialist I have used pistols and rifles extensively.

People mostly want to know what you based your training on and what experience you have. It is good for someone to ask because their life depends on the training they will receive from an instructor. You need to know that the person who is teaching you actually has experience in real combat. What does the person teaching you have to draw from as an instructor if he has no experience? Without a penchant for training in combat you won't have the will to succeed – you need a certain disposition that predisposes you to this.

In 1992 I developed an interest in Close Protection (CP), which was a very new occupation in the public sector in South Africa at the time. There was not much in the way of sophisticated training courses for civilians. So whenever there was a possibility to train with an instructor that knew what he was talking about, we would jump at the opportunity. During the period 1992 till 2005 I attended 4 separate CP courses and a number of other related courses such as shooting in low light, advanced foot and vehicle drills, Improvised Explosive Devices (IED) recognition, unarmed combat, knife fighting, and numerous other skills and courses not mentioned here. These instructors ranged from civilian instructors to ex Special Forces (SF) and FBI certified instructors. During my CP experience, I have looked after celebrities, businessmen, royalty and diplomats.

I was able to apply IED recognition experience in counter terrorism operations. In 2000 I was tasked to come up with a plan to minimize IEDs being placed in the V&A Waterfront Cape Town.

South Africa has a tradition of hunters and shooters because of the nature of the land and its tumultuous history over the last 300 years, where hunting and fighting were the order of the day, and this gave most South Africans a good taste of reality in combat. Therefore, it was more likely that we would be exposed to weapons living in South Africa.

In the military we dealt with all sorts of weapons and equipment, such as radar and radio communications etc. High threat CP is commonly referred to as Private Security Detail (PSD), and during 2004 the conflict in Iraq attracted a lot of PSD operators from all over the world. Having military experience and about 15 years in CP by that time, I decided it would benefit my overall abilities to get some PSD experience and training.

You soon learn it takes a determined, focused and deliberate mindset balanced with self confidence that will allow you to win in a real gunfight; there is no room for negative thoughts or thoughts that detract from the winning, orientated and focused mind.

When you train for combat in reality it helps to train instinctively and to train so you react and don't have to think about tactics because there is only time for reacting.

My experience with martial and unarmed combat spans about 38 years where I trained not just with Karate systems but also to a minor degree Aikido (which is not a self-defense system), Judo and some ground fighting. My weapons training was with various weapon systems, handguns and rifles etc. which spans about 30 years.

To better understand where my skill level was in terms of international standards, I did an advanced certificate in handgun and rifle skills to round off my weapons qualifications. This certifies a person to teach to an advanced level anywhere in the world and is internationally recognized. From approximately 1994/97 I started to develop the mobility shooting drills for handgun and rifle which you can now see on YouTube and also on Patreon see below.

- https://www.patreon.com/ITC_za
- https://www.amazon.com/Basic-Elite-Level-Handgun-Training/dp/B0851KJKZT
- https://www.amazon.com/Personal-Protection-Body-Guarding-manual-ebook/dp/B07DY84XPX

During this period, I got most of my Close Protection experience and was tasked as team leader about 70 times or more. In the period 1990-1991 I studied physical education which has helped me better understand the body and how it functions. I apply this in my unarmed combat and weapons training courses.

Basic rifle fighting skills

Having covered the above skills focusing on basic weapon hand line, now we consider how to fight with the rifle:

1. **Weapon manipulation** skills as mentioned above.
2. **Shooting and movement**: this would include shooting on the move and or covering fire, which sometimes requires the operator to move to a position that allows them to give covering fire from an appropriate angle.
3. **Correct use of cover** will include but not limited to shooting around cover, best from of cover, moving from cover to cover. This can be difficult because most people that will do sports shooting will for the sake of efficiency lose respect for good cover and end up making bad cover practice and subconscious actions.
4. **Reaction to incoming fire** e.g., type of action (response) and speed of action (reflexes) and this could be to neutralize an attacker or attack the ambush itself.
5. **How to break contact** using assault and heavy fire on enemy and dissuade them from following and then attacking you again. This can but doesn't need to include anti tracking and E&E but those would be good skills to have too.
6. **How to stay calm when under fire**: this is the hardest to teach as it comes more from experience when in combat, having a good system of mindset training exercise can help but will have limited effect until you change your 'internal mental tape loop' from one of fear to excitement (if this is necessary).

Basics you need to survive once you have the above aspects mastered:

1. **Fitness** and personal movement skills, using tactical

movement and **stealth** – these are skills needed to survive a battle field etc.

2. Personal **camouflage**, this includes uniform and face paint, camouflage of your hide OP/LP (observation post listening post) and dugout.
3. Equipment camouflage and method of carrying personal equipment (backpack/chest webbing/belt webbing). This is important because it dictates how much and what you can carry. If the load bearing vest is capable of carrying heavy loads you tend to load it up with stuff you don't necessarily need.
4. **Caches and resupply** around your area of operations.
5. Short- and long-term **planning** for operations and survival purposes.

Basics of survival once you have the above:

1. **Shelters and cover**: fast and expedient forms of cover, both natural and manmade, done with efficiency. Efficiency is a lot easier than it would have been 100 years ago, because modern materials are light and strong and allow fast shelter deployment.
2. **Fire and cooking**: all methods of fire making is essential as is making water safe to drink, and cooking food properly is essential.
3. **Finding water and food**: natural foods in the wild, including medicines.
4. **Navigation**: compass or GPS, traveling through the landscape efficiently and safely.
5. **Basic medical**.

Shooting stance for light caliber weapons

One type of stance if you are using a low recoil rifle such as MP5 or 5.56 caliber weapon is to stand relatively square on to a target as this will allow you to move around more easily as well as center the weapon target more easily. Have one leg slightly behind to keep you stable for shooting multiple shots in succession, **arms tucked in, especially the right arm should be tucked if you are a right-handed shooter (less exposure to enemy fire); feet shoulder width apart or wider,** lean slightly forward about 15 to 20 degrees (to absorb recoil better). Body weight is in the middle of your feet always; your weight should be balanced **50/50 when not shooting so you can move quickly** in any applicable direction.

If the front of your weapon pushes up (lifts during recoil) too easily then consider a better compensator or suppressor that helps keep the muzzle lift down and cuts down muzzle blast at the same time. To maintain a balanced stance and head posture you will need to bring the stock closer to the centerline so you don't have to look for the front sight by moving your head side to side or up and down. When using a low caliber (low recoiling) rifle in and around cover as you might end up ***exposing yourself a bit too much*** but this can be mitigated by placing the weapon on the shoulder (outside of the deltoid muscle), as this lowers the profile of your overall target area. This is used in cornering around solid cover such as walls, vehicles and any other large solid cover.

This stance applies even more so if you are using an armored vehicle, as the sides of your body are not covered by the plates that stop rifle rounds. You therefore rely on the plates for frontal protection and the vehicle for side protection. Consider that you might not want to place your feet on the ground because the bullets that have deflected off the ground will track low along the ground at about 4-6 inches.

Shooting stance for heavier caliber weapons

This stance is for a heavier caliber such as the 7.62 weapons that have a slight bit more recoil. It can also be used for semi auto rifles with lesser calibers and therefore less recoil. Here you will need to have one foot back and one forward such as in a martial stance such as karate or boxer's stance. The upper body will always be similar depending on the length of the stock and the type of weapon being using such as either a rifle or submachine gun (SMG). You lean slightly forward to compensate for recoil but you don't want to fall forward.

You use your **whole posture** to point your weapon in the direction of the target, as this allows you to fire without aiming if the attacker is close enough to you. You will be facing the correct direction then you pick up the sights and aim (this happens in seconds or less). Hold close to the magazine as it helps to control the weapon; do not use this hold with an M16 rifle as you may have feeding problems (this might be ironed out as time goes on because of improvements to the weapon system). If you lean too far forward then you might decrease some of your mobility and if you don't lean forward enough you don't control the recoil, so find a balance.

Important note: keep in mind each person is built differently and some stances are more comfortable for some than for others. Be flexible as long as it does not affect the integrity of the stance which should be balanced to allow good movement.

Basic shooting stances

At a basic level the person only needs to be able to execute the following techniques listed below slowly with **100% correct technique or close to it over a period of a few months,** do not expect speed or even accuracy. Focus on doing things deliberately, especially the things that matter later on in the person's shooting training that allow for speed and accuracy. This will be balance, good control over the weapon, firm but relaxed grip, good sight picture with a relaxed upper body (shoulders and neck).

Make sure the safety procedures are addressed and adhered to with no exceptions because this is where the student needs to develop a good understanding of *where to place the finger when not shooting,* and to put the safety on when not engaged in shooting. Insist on safety first – no speed and or accuracy yet. Speed and other intensity exercises will only be addressed after months of training 2-4 hours per week end over 6 months.

Shooting Standing

Going forward and backwards as well as lateral movement.

High profile shooting position: this can be standing almost straight, either feet together or as in the combat stance with one foot behind. This might be dictated by the power of the caliber you are using – if your feet are together then you might be pushed back too much and accuracy suffers. The 223-semi auto rifle or 9mm carbine shouldn't trouble you if you are leaning slightly forward, but you find with multiple fast shots this can happen where the weapon lifts due to cumulative recoil from quick, successive shots.

High profile with lateral movement: the same body position as mentioned above is easier to move in if your feet are shoulder width apart next to each other.

Low profile: this is for combat shooting when you can't take cover. You lower your overall profile to present a lesser target area for the enemy while maintaining a good mobility platform to move fast off. This helps both shooting and mobility and to lower your profile.

Low profile with lateral movement: this takes a lot of core strength and agility, also good abductors and adductor muscles help, as well as opening and closing the legs. It's very stable and a good platform to shoot from while being a slightly smaller target yourself.

Kneeling

How you hold and turn the body is going to be important when kneeling; the position of your knees and upper body flexibility will dictate how far you can turn your legs as seen in picture sequences below. The bracing (left) arm holding the fore grip goes over the knee, not on it. This allows more control and less movement in the weapon; in this position you can lean a bit more forward.

1. High profile kneeling (standard kneeling for rifle shooting)
2. Low profile kneeling

Lying prone

Lying and rolling sideways and crawling forward or backwards becomes the predominant movement or position of a combatant. Some people like to bring the one leg up for easier breathing as it lifts the chest slightly but this is only important if you are not fit enough and trained to control your breathing. The lying position will be determined by the context of your function for example if in a PSD situation then you will most probably be standing 98% of the time, in the context of a soldier you could find yourself in a lying position more often depending on the battle conditions. Your function will also dictate what position you will be in predominantly, such as a sniper or designated marksman will also spend most of their time in a prone position once in a combat zone (if not patrolling or reaching an OP then you will walk). For combat functions such as standard infantry or PSD or maybe survival (civil unrest) when using your rifle will require less equipment than a designated marksman or sniper so getting up from the ground will be less of a hassle.

When lying on your back, shooting from between the legs is slightly safer than with a pistol as your rifle barrel will normally extend out beyond the legs which have been pulled up. This shooting position is used very little in real combat so doesn't have to be practiced extensively.

Getting up from prone

This is getting up without using your hands and you still need to aim at the target(s) in the event you need to react to them either moving or shooting at you. This allows you to fire at any stage of the getting up process, which is important for any real combat environment. If you don't have good core strength then this becomes a difficult technique to execute, core is the strength in the abdominals and obliques and to some extent the hip flexors as well.

The correct "getting up from prone" technique is as done on the pistol course: the leg action remains the same and upper body lean as well; it's just the rifle in the hands that change when doing this type of movement. There is more weight going forward with a rifle than a pistol, so it should be easier. The context of this movement is more for combat and when the enemy are close (see below for both pistol and rifle).

Getting up with a pistol

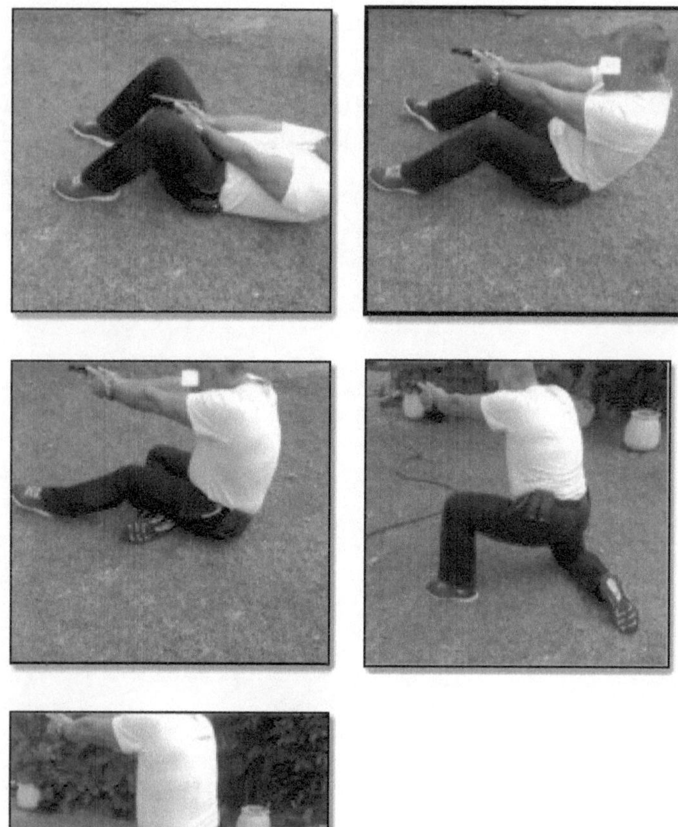

Getting up with a rifle

Shooting from "low ready" position

Note the stock is closer to the centerline than normal.

This shooting position allows a more relaxed stance with the rifle coming up to the eye and you don't have to look for the sights as they should come up in front of your eye naturally given your structure. This stance has less neck tension and if you keep your right arm close to your body it makes you a smaller target area. The closer to the centerline your stock is the more weight there is behind the weapon and it's less likely to move sideways during rapid fire. If you push a person shoulder it's easier to move than if you push on the center of their body. The squarer your body is the less likely the weapon is to slide sideways. You can also use what is called a "horse stance" in Karate where your feet are next to each other but wide apart. This doesn't allow as much recoil control but is fast and can be effective.

Ready stance

Best stance for recoil control. Notice the weapon is close to centerline.

Horse stance

Feet parallel but fairly wide for stability and bending forward to compensate for recoil, this works well (sufficiently) for *low recoiling semi auto rifles* like 5.56x45 (223):

Standing shooting while supported

The following description is only one way of many and it's up to you to adapt according to your knowledge and understanding as well as experience what type of support structure you use for your rifle. Shooting supported does lend itself to accuracy and should be taken up when possible. This will only be used when you have time and need accuracy; this is normally when the enemy is at 300 meters and more and only displays a small target area:

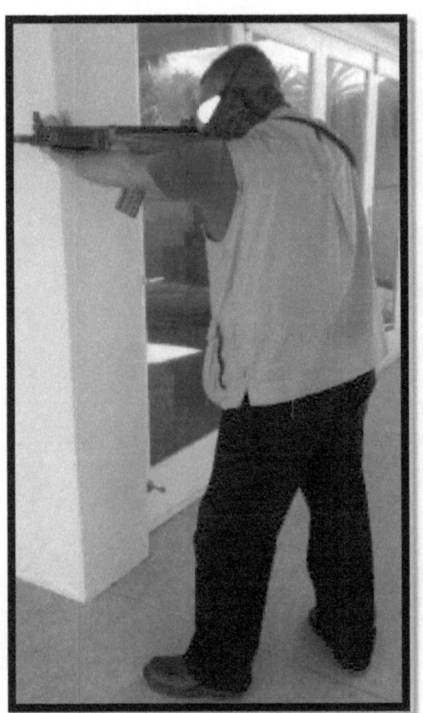 

Weapon presentation

The images below highlight technical aspects, from the side to facing forward. The right foot can move forward as this puts you in a good balanced stance for a stable shooting platform. The right arm is tucked in to keep the overall size of your target profile to the enemy small, the left hand drives the weapon but should be mostly only hold the rifle because most of the movement should be done with the core muscles, which are the abdominal, oblique's (internal and external), and transverse abdominis. To be efficient you only need to move the one foot which in this case is the right foot forward and this should give you a stable stance. Crouching more than is demonstrated will give you more recoil control for small caliber semi-auto rifles.

Advanced level shooting positions

For the advanced level shooter, the person only needs to be able to do the firing positions described below, and in a one-dimensional function (meaning multiple directions do not necessarily have to be addressed in the section, but can be if the person wants to develop quickly). The change from one position to another should be fast and fluid, going into the correct position naturally. This includes aiming with the whole body, balanced, slightly leaning forward, both eyes open, the weapon should be firmly in the shoulder as close under the aiming eye as possible, which is normally close to the sternum. Normally a wide stance is more stable and can be applied here but for striking it can inhibit you from striking properly so make sure you can transform the stance for different disciplines appropriately.

The advanced shooter should be able to shoot a bit faster with **accuracy** and therefore the person's safety should be very natural and second nature to prevent accidents from happening while using the weapon. This is normally accomplished by keeping the finger off the trigger till you are ready to shoot.

The advanced shooter *should not have to think about remedial action* such as stoppage drills as this means they are still at the basic to intermediate level. Therefore, the stoppage drills for an advanced shooter should be well understood and executed efficiently.

1. **Standing**: needs good forward and backwards stability and movement as well as lateral movement because the person should be able to do movement subconsciously to keep their focus on accuracy. That means looking at a moving target (real combat) and the operator should be aware of the condition of the weapon they are carrying and be able to shoot comfortably in same positions as for Basic Level earlier above.
2. **Kneeling**: as for Basic Level above plus:
    ◦ Kneeling with both knees on the ground. This can be very stable but you will need to be fit to hold the rifle up.
3. **Squatting position**: this is quick down and quick to recover from the kneeling to standing, used when moving in and around cover. This is done the same way as you do a deep squat during resistance exercise.
4. **Sitting with arms braced** on knees (see picture below).
5. **Lying Prone**: as for Basic Level plus:
    ◦ Lying on the side: this is a shooting position practiced in a lot of courses lately but in real combat it's maybe only going to be used 1-2% of the time (e.g., where you are shooting under a vehicle or some

other low structure) if at all and therefore spending hours drilling this will be a waste of time when you could be doing intensity drills instead.

This would be considered a low-profile shooting position in kneeling:

Sitting with arms braced on knees (you could hold the stock closer to your centerline which will give you more recoil control):

Elite level shooting positions

For the Elite level shooter, the operator needs to be able to do the following firing positions in combination and in tactical scenarios as well as highly mobile shooting exercises. The person's accuracy and weapons alignment should be without thought at this stage and their accuracy should be at a high-level combined with speed.

This is the level where the student can address all the tactical aspects of shooting as in multiple aspects skill drills, such as barrier use or correct use of cover, with additional areas of skill done in succession such as movement, shooting from cover, stoppage drills, point aim and aimed shots interspersed and if team drills are being trained then team drills can be addressed now.

Shooting positions and probability of use when patrolling: the stance you will mostly use to engage the enemy will be either **standing** or standing **low profile** or lying down in **prone**, these 3 stances are used about 90% of the time and should drilled to perfection (performed) till you can shoot from them with ease.

1. **Standing**: the stationary aspects should have been mastered by now so the focus can be on forward and backwards movement as well as lateral movement, training to move with a gliding movement with the feet sliding over the ground as this will allow you to shoot better while moving. This does take good movement skills practice.
   a. **High profile** standing shooting position exercises
      i. From facing forward moving to facing left
      ii. From facing forward moving to facing right
      iii. From facing forward moving to facing backwards, move feet as little as possible
   b. **Low profile** standing shooting position: this is most likely the position to choose for combat. It's more likely you will want to get low and it is an **autonomic response** to incoming enemy fire. You will either drop or take a very low profile, while looking for cover. This is a natural human response and therefore using this reaction and building on it is a good idea:
      i. From facing forward to facing left
      ii. From facing forward to facing right
      iii. From facing forward to facing backwards: this is not likely to happen unless you are surrounded, but movement skills are important so having this skill is good.
2. **Kneeling**: as for Basic Level with extra directional

applications. Personally, I don't suggest you use the kneeling stance because of the reasons mentioned in the manual, but it is useful if you have a little cover or a depression:

    a. High profile kneeling (standard kneeling for rifle shooting)

        i. From facing forward to facing left

        ii. From facing forward to facing right

        iii. From facing forward to facing backwards

    b. Low profile kneeling

        i. From facing forward to facing left

        ii. From facing forward to facing right

        iii. From facing forward to facing backwards

    c. Kneeling on both knees

        i. From facing forward to facing left

        ii. From facing forward to facing right

        iii. From facing forward to facing backwards

3. **Squatting** position:

    i. From facing forward to facing left

    ii. From facing forward to facing right

4. **Lying prone**: as for Advanced Level plus:

    a. Lying on the stomach

        i. Rolling left, shoot 1 shot; normally this exercise can be repeated 5 times in total

        ii. Rolling right, 1 shot; again, 5 repeats

    b. Lying on the back:

        i. Roll onto stomach and fire; repeat exercise firing from back and stomach 5 times

    c. Lying on the side:

        i. Use this is when you are lying on your side shooting under a vehicle or barrier. Fire 5 rounds. This is a very low mobility shooting position so it should be used wisely as to not compromise your ability to take cover, move to a position of advantage or just move out of the immediate area. ***Keep in mind you might never use this position in combat so don't do hours of training on these positions, 90 % of your training should be standing and low-profile shooting positions.***

ii. Turn onto stomach, shoot 1 shot (focus on breathing and sights even if the target is close by because breathing while lying is very disruptive to sighting).

iii. Turn onto back, shoot 1 shot. This means you will be shooting upside down, so ***make sure it's done in a safe manner***, take your time.

The above transitions will challenge your movement skills and your core muscles. This is where you can also add in some drills where you get up from the ground without putting your hands on the ground (see earlier picture sequence about getting up from the ground).

High kneeling (you will notice the stock is close to the centerline):

Low kneeling with the spine being about 30-degree forward bend will help you to control the recoil:

Posture, Aiming, And Trigger Control

The following points will apply to semi auto and full auto rifles as well as carbines (PDW). The techniques can apply to larger calibers such as semi auto 308 caliber rifles if the recoil impulse is low, due to a suppressor or muzzle break (beware muzzle breaks can be debilitating if you have team mates to your side because they make the rifle report very loud to people standing beside you).

Posture (Stance)

This is your position for pointing your entire body at the target as you look for and or look at your target. Use your core muscles to make finer adjustments. Don't try engage and move your weapon with your arm muscles because they are not strong enough to move the rifle fast and stop on target efficiently when needed with precision.

1. Use a fighting stance: one foot forward, one foot back, shoulder width apart, normally it will be the left foot forward and right foot back for right-handed shooters. This will allow you to lean forward without falling over as your base (lower body structure) is large. This stance can apply to all martial techniques where a good base is needed.
2. Lean slightly forward, as the forward posture *controls* the *recoil impulse* better which means you have to fight the weapon less and the weight of your body allows for this.
3. Bring the weapon up to a natural and comfortable position, putting it closer on the pectoral muscle will allow more control over the weapon because the recoil is directed down closer to your centerline. This shorter line between the rifle stock and the center of your weight and spine (centerline) means more weight behind the weapon. Your weapon stock

will need to be short enough to do this. You can see this positioning line as a mid-clavicle line roughly on the nipple for anatomical purposes.

4. Stay fairly square to the target (i.e., hips facing the target) if the **length of the stock** allows this, to facilitate more natural movement and bring the weapon naturally under your right eye if you are right-handed shooter. If you are left eye dominant but shoot right-handed, then the sights will be placed under your left eye.

5. Look at the target first because you need to **ID whether the target is friend or foe**, your target can be your attacker so you need to identify what your next move will be: shooting or shoot while moving or move then stop and shoot. You should also be tracking the target if it is running/moving, as keeping your eyes up is important for location and tracking of the enemy.

Low-profile stance

When you use a low-profile shooting position you don't lean forward, you just drop down into the position with your body as parallel to the ground as possible, without causing too much fatigue. Hopefully any enemy contact will be over quickly and you can stand up and run to cover. A low-profile stance is more for a quick contact and where **longer-range shots are needed and where no cover is available.** Benefits:

a. You are quicker off the mark (movement)
b. Better overall mobility
c. Faster to move to next position than when in kneeling position
d. You give a lower profile of a target than when kneeling
e. You won't get hit in the femoral artery as easy as when

kneeling

f. You can move laterally if needed, unlike kneeling you are stationery and can't move

Comparison with target size when in a low-profile shooting position:

Weapon alignment

Use your whole body to aim: body posture is part of your aiming if it's done correctly. This must be relaxed but stable, bent knees, concertinaed down **not leaning forward** too far as this will put you off balance and you will therefore not be able to move forward quickly. If you are using the stance of one foot forward and one back as in picture demonstration then you can lean a bit more forward than you would normally.

Lifting the weapon to your eyes must be practiced so it comes to the **same position every time**. This is not always possible in close quarter fighting but for accuracy it helps to engage the targets faster. This means bringing the weapon up to your eyes and not leaning your head forward too much as this can lead to fatigue compared with a relaxed natural head position.

When lifting a bull-pup type rifle the weapon can be kept close to your centerline for fast shooting. Where you look is where you will shoot, especially when point aiming (point aim is appropriate for ranges of 5 to 20 meters roughly, depending on your skill level).

1. Practice from a *standing posture* weapon alignment and position (see picture). Standing and prone are the two shooting positions that you will use 95% of the time and should be practiced predominantly to be good at rifle combat.

2. Bring the stock up on the pectoral muscle so the weapon sights are below your eyes. It is much closer to the sternum (also called sternal border) than most butt stock shooting placement. This allows your body weight to absorb recoil because it is closer to the centerline. When it is placed on the shoulder there is less weight to absorb recoil.

3. Don't tilt your head if you can help it as this will **affect** your **depth perception** and **peripheral vision,** and will restrict your movement slightly as it will imbalance your centerline. Keep in mind your body will follow your head movement. Bad head positions usually result from poorly fitted rifles, so if you're having problems getting a natural head alignment, try to adjust your stock accordingly.

4. The ***stock length must allow your weapon sights to come up automatically to between your eyes*** so you don't have to look for your sights, the stock is sometimes adjusted a little shorter than normal to allow for this specific stance, but if it is very short your eye will be very close the front sight when in prone (lying down), so practice both standing and prone to get a comfortable stock length for natural sighting.

When turning you should keep this structure as much as possible with a relaxed disposition, and focus on moving the whole body without adjusting any of your weapon positioning.

Sight picture (aiming)

Here "sight picture" means what you see when the sights are aligned on the target. This is dependent on the type of weapon sights, for simplicity we will focus on the iron sights most weapons come with.

For the sights to be used correctly you need to have your eye the correct distance (eye relief) from the first circle if you use the R4/ Galil type sights. **Eye relief** (distance from your eye to the rear sight aperture) is important for circular iron sights as well as scopes. The stock must allow a comfortable eye relief; a relaxed head position should allow many minutes on the sights comfortably. This could mean shortening the stock if possible; this will also allow quicker sight acquisition, if it is too far from your face you have to move your face forward and causes neck strain and slow sight alignment. Some people use a larger aperture and then get used to this as it allows them to see more of the downrange target area and pick up the front sight quicker.

For weapons that have a circle rear sight and a circle around the front pin you need to bring your eye close enough to the rear aperture so that **both circles are the same size** and in line. This sometimes means shortening the stock of the weapon.

By comparison, a 'V' shaped rear sight is the same as aiming with a pistol – just line up the front and back and if the sight is set properly, you will hit the target.

In some situation in countries where the weapons were bought second hand you might need to adjust the sights or even fix them as it's very possible, they will be broken or damaged.

If the sights are set in at about 200-300 meters for the 5.56 x45 caliber then you're placing your **front sights on** the intended point of bullet impact when you are shooting from 0 to 300 meters. That means a 55-grain standard 5.56 bullet doing 2700 fps will give you a maximum height of the cone of flight being 4.3-5 inches above the point of aim and the drop will be -9 inches at 400 meters (roughly).

When shooting in combat, pull the trigger when you are on target – don't hesitate, the longer you wait the less accuracy you get. You will never get a perfect sight picture in combat so practice for a good sight picture, balancing speed with accuracy. For quick shooting close in with reasonable accuracy don't try to put the reticule/front sight post on the target – just put the **frame of the sighting device** over the target. This means the circular front site on the LM 4/5/6/Galil.

Accuracy guide for US army and FBI:

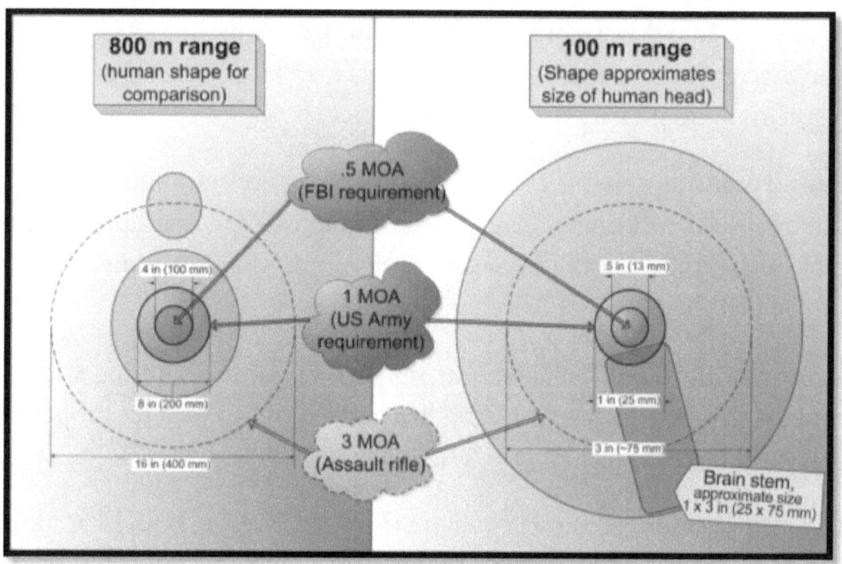

Trigger control

Use the tip of your trigger finger. Some people can use the whole finger for combat accuracy and still get good shots on target so don't be too pedantic when it comes to trigger control for combat (compare with sniper rifle technique where you can get stricter with trigger control).

Pull straight back – pulling on the trigger to either side will cause a slight deviation in accuracy.

The term **"follow through"** refers to keeping the weapon on target for a split second after the shot, and is obviously not necessary if you are shooting multiple targets as fast as possible, but it can help shooters improve their accuracy.

Trigger reset should be applied so that the full movement of the trigger is not engaged again, as the trigger is ready to go after the reset i.e., don't allow your trigger finger to get too far off the trigger as the weapon is cycling, as it means your next shot is delayed because the trigger finger has further to come back onto the trigger.

When shooting prone, typically at long range, really emphasize the tip of the finger, unless you are shooting fast at close range and just want reasonable accuracy. And take 3 deep fast breaths and fire at the end of your third breath. Do NOT HOLD YOUR BREATH in combat as this will incapacitate you, as aerobic exercise requires oxygen and any lack of oxygen will cause your muscles to fatigue, muscle fatigue will cause your brain to falter due to feeling lighted headed. Prone shooting can inhibit your breathing somewhat, so ensure you have adequate breathing throughout the engagement.

Accuracy at long ranges is more difficult because any movement that is unnecessary when pulling the trigger will cause the weapon to be off target. Condition yourself to **pull the trigger as you are on target** for fast target acquisition and quick shots, which will be the case in a battle situation.

Target acquisition

In reality, you could say that there are three types of shooting situations where you need to acquire the target:

1. **Fast:** this is the 0-to-10-meter range where **point aim** techniques apply, because most fast shooting is in close range. Breathing discipline doesn't matter except to breathe into the stomach, focus on mindset and relaxation. Keep referring

back to your body position and overall stance and technique.

1. **Fast and accurate**: the intermediate range where the target is at about 50 to 200 meters and the **battle is dynamic** and acquiring the targets *fast and accurately* is more necessary.

This is where using the two-circle aperture are lined up and the same size, instead of only using the front circle or front pin/post sights i.e., for more accuracy at these ranges, you need to pay more attention to your sight picture.

The success of this is determined by keeping the same body alignment and head with the rifle, giving your brain a quick point of reference for fast target acquisition.

1. **Accurate**: precision shooting where you use the sights to the full extent with breathing, trigger control, and follow through. This is when your targets are out to 300 or more meters or you are in a sniper role for the fighting unit.

Technically you could say there is a 4th acquisition type which is fast target acquisition with movement but most people don't train it and I haven't seen anybody move fast and still hit head shots. So, you could say that would be the 4th but we won't include it as it's too difficult to explain the dynamics of it and is better taught in person.

Point aiming technique

Because with all close-range engagements, time is of the essence and you need to take into consideration, you might not be able to bring the rifle up to your face as you would normally do. Therefore, you need "point aim" technique to get reasonable accuracy.

This might be more difficult with a bull pup design but it is quite easy with rifles like the South African R4/5/6 or LM.

The context for this technique is 0 to 5 or even 10 or 20 meters if you train for accuracy when shooting instinctively. Consider including point aiming technique in quite a lot of your training so that you have confidence when engaging the enemy at close range. This will be especially pertinent for urban fighting in and around houses and buildings. Most of your training should be fast close-range shooting.

Where these close-range engagements will normally happen is:

- In front of crowds with the weapon held in "relaxed ready".
- In houses: all urban type conflicts where you have the rifle in low ready and the ranges are 0-5 or even 10 meters with training.
- Guarding, where people approach to gain access to a facility, is where the low ready is used.
- Doing PSD type operations, where you are escorting a principal with a rifle and a side arm.

Close range point aiming

Close range point aim can be applied in different scenarios. Shown below are the types of point aim that apply:

If you are standing in low ready and have a close target (1 to 10 meters):

The technique:

1. Because the rifle is already in a side on position to your body and only needs to be lifted, doing any ***unnecessary movement*** will ***slow you down*** and allow your enemy more time to engage you, so keeping the orientation and just lifting and shooting is the fastest way to engage a close target.
2. Lift the rifle past your neck to about chin level, note the barrel is under the aiming eye (see pictures below).
3. Use the barrel as a point of reference for aiming, the target is so close you can't miss, as this is not a shooting technique for longer than about 5-8 or maybe 10 meters, depending on how you train it and use it.

See pictures below picture 1 and 2 (the low ready and presenting rifle as shown below from back and front view):

Picture 1

Picture 2

Low-profile point aiming

This next example is for close range, either coming through a low obstacle or you just got up from kneeling as well as other scenarios where you come out of a low stance. This can be applied in a situation where speed and accuracy is needed but the enemy is fairly close and you need to observe the surroundings while you engage the targets of opportunity. Here you are aligned with the weapon but you are not using the sights only your body position and is good for people out to 10 meters depending on your training:

Below is the best way to point aim for intermediate ranges 10-50 meters, this is also the technique I will use most of the time. That is because it is the most accurate way of pointing because you can refer to the sights when needed and therefore is the most versatile aiming technique. This also applies to the low-profile standing position, because you are still pointing with your whole body and the technique is the same as for standing upright as seen below:

The angle will
allow force of
recoil to go into
ground

Below is shown the **least effective way to point aim** (normally the only way to get hits with this stance is to walk the rounds onto the target). The weakness is because of the alignment (the weapon is off to the side and thus not under the eye). This position can be accurate but only with a lot of training so if training large groups of people it is more expedient to teach techniques that are easier to learn:

Shooting Exercises

Aiming your rifle instinctively

The objective of the following aiming exercises is to help develop the skills and accuracy aspect of aiming with a good structure that allows the person to *instinctively position the weapon for a quick shot*. Shooting structure is applied to both handgun and rifle and differs slightly in the upper body position but the stance can remain fairly similar if the rifle caliber is small. This initial stance must be drilled to instinct and must be stable and relaxed to allow natural aiming, the more efficient the stance and aiming is the less energy you use and the more you can engage the enemy without tensing up. This is essential for coping with the stress and being able to engage multiple times without fatigue. This is ideal but keep in mind that real combat doesn't always allow a good shooting platform; normally you would have to see the enemy beforehand to be able to engage with a good stance and shooting platform. The stress and the speed with which targets can appear will normally cause the sight picture and aiming to be very quick and fleeting.

Basic drills for aiming

This drill is called *weapon presentation* (aiming) where the whole body is aligned from the stance to the points of contact of the hand and face on the rifle. Once this is mastered then acquiring the target will be easier as your eyes will look through the weapon sights onto the target and every aspect is aligned as practiced. This should be done relaxed and comfortable to allow easy and faster target acquisition.

Exercise 1

These drills should ideally be done at least every 3rd to 5th training session to ingrain the basics of aiming over a period of six months if the students train over a year period. This might sound long but there is no quick solution, so to be efficient you need to have the correct technique.

The target is at about **10 meters** from the student. For a good outcome to this exercise, breathe deep while doing the drills and stay relaxed as much as possible. Controlling your breathing to integrate with actual shots taken is only for long range shots while lying down otherwise you must learn to breathe into your lower stomach. Each stage has a different focus but they build onto each other so it is important to do each stage individually.

1. **Stance** drills: **finding the relaxed and correct posture** immediately. Do 20 to 40 repetitions; too many and the person will get tired and do them incorrectly. Don't worry about where the weapon is at this point in time. Focus on the overall feeling of the stance and pointing at a target with the whole body. Lift the rifle and look at the target, check where the barrel is compared to the target and keep this up till the pointing is going well enough to be in the right place without effort and conscious thought.
    a. The reason for this is when you look at an object and then focus your whole body to orientate your weapon and sights
    b. Your body should move as a unit because you want to aim with your body and then look for the sights and your target, this will make you more efficient
    c. When your whole body moves to orientate towards the enemy then you can more easily sight your weapon and control recoil more efficiently
2. **Weapon <u>alignment</u>** drills: here you bring the weapon up **to the same point** each time and try to *feel the <u>points of contact</u> on the face shoulder and hands.* This is done for 20 to 40 repetitions, **keep relaxed** and focus on your overall stance. This is very important for further shooting excellence and *fast target acquisition.* Now you can focus more on the actual aiming of the weapon, by this I mean not aiming with sights but *with alignment.*

This will also teach the brain what the *correct alignment* is and *eye relief* for fast target acquisition. Once all the points of contact are achieved simultaneously and constantly you will find that your sights just pop up in front of your eyes.

Being more an emphasis on just looking through the sights than actually acquiring a target, this exercise is about eye relief and finding the sights, not actually using the sights to aim.

1. **Targeting** drills: here, the focus is on actually *acquiring the target itself.* This can only be natural if the stance and weapon alignment are correct. This is important because later on you want to improve on the speed with which you can see the sights and engage the target. Don't hold the fore grip too tight.

Start with the correct mindset, as this helps to keep you relaxed, keep the same position of the upper body as much as possible. Smoothly and quickly find the target but don't do it at a pace (speed) that will tense you up as this is counterproductive to speed later on when you are advanced. Speed can cause certain upper body muscles to tense up and the whole emphasis is on relaxation.

a. Bring up the weapon so you can see the sights without looking for them.
b. Don't fire dry or live yet. Do 20 to 40 repetitions.
c. Now you can do 20-40 dry fire
d. Then apply single shot live fire keeping all aspects accurate, smooth and focused. Do anything from 5 shots to 20 depending on your budget and or if you are military then do 20 shots.
e. For the more advanced, shooters you can have focus targets which are small that can be engaged with either one or

"double tap" (2 quick shots) trying to keep the shots as close to each other as possible. Start with 10 meters as this is a drill not a tactic.

f. Once you are comfortable with this you can increase distance 20 to 40 meters; for small targets this will be really challenging.

1. **Trigger control:** doing stance, weapon alignment, target acquisition drills together and ***dry fire as you come on target***, make sure you don't pull the weapon out of alignment when you pull the trigger. Allow a second or 2 on the target so you don't pull it out of alignment. This is not as important for a semi auto rifle that are used in a combat situation because the range doesn't allow you to miss a large target at ranges like 20 to 50 meters (out 100 meters).

    a. Knowing the pressure and feel of the trigger is good, and will be known by a person that is puts effort into to spending time feeling the pressure and break of the trigger. For an assault rifle this is not as important as it would be for a precision sniper system.

    b. Here the finger placement is not as important as when doing precision shooting over 300 meters most probably lying down. The trigger can be depressed without too much consideration to placement, as the ranges of combat when using an assault rifle are normally close-range targets such as 5 meters out to 300 meters.

    c. Try to keep the feeling you had of ***correct alignment*** of body, rifle and how you acquired the sights, the position of your cheek. This can be helped by putting a piece of material that indicates your cheek position by feel. This helps to have a similar feeling as you take up the weapon to aim.

    d. Hold your weapon firmly in your grip, tight to the shoulder **but not too tight** that it causes tension and shaking

    e. Focus purely on trigger control

    f. Focus on trigger and then reset

    g. Fire live 5 shots

2. **Combination drills:** do all the above aspects with one shot *live fire*, for 10 repetitions. This is done to combine all the areas practiced above together as a combined exercise. This now is going to be challenging if the above aspects are not fully integrated into your subconscious yet. You will see excellent accuracy at this point if you have done the above exercises for over 3 months 2 hours a day once over a weekend.

    a. Combinations such, as shoot one shot for accuracy then do movement with stoppage drill. Or incorporate a magazine change into the movement. This is quite complicated and demanding, especially if it's dynamic.

    b. It could also be an accuracy drill, then a barrier followed by a stoppage drill. ***Don't focus on speed***, it should always be focused on *technique* and *efficiency* to get the best out the exercise.

        i. Remember this is a drill for **standing** and **<u>quick target acquisition</u>**, it is not for lying down in prone

    c. The target is at

        i. 10 meters for the basic students

        ii. 20 meters for the advanced students

        iii. 30-40 meters for elite students

d. REST 5 minutes, do another 5 to 10 repetitions 1 shot at a time, patience and deliberate training will benefit you in the long run so don't rush things.

e. REST 5 minutes do another 5 to 10 repetitions, this time you might want to add a bit of speed and intensity. If you are new, don't push the parameters yet, still go at a pace you feel comfortable.

TOTAL OF 15 to 30 rounds expended on this exercise, but it is up to the instructor to decide what the intensity is and how much ammunition is expended.

Advanced drills for aiming

Exercise 2

Increased distances with same focus on technique (now from 10 moving to 20 meters).

This is working from a standing posture. It is important that the student be in a balanced stance for the movement drills to work properly and to be effective. The target is at **20 meters** from the operator, and many drills are then as they were Basic Level above, but now at the longer 20m range and some have variations:

1. **Stance** drills: as for Basic Level.
2. **Weapon alignment** drills: as for Basic Level.
3. **Targeting** drills: as for Basic Level, except here you might want to put up 2 or 3 targets so that you can transition from target to target.
4. **Trigger control:** as for Basic Level.
5. **Side stepping** drills (**stepping sideways is for fairly close-range targets**): the focus is on a target at **about 20 meters**

from the operator, the distance can be increased as the student becomes more competent. For more advanced students you can have a target at 40 meters and for advanced to Elite level shooters 50-60 meters. It is important to not lose any of the previous skills developed in points 1-4. You could even do these drills every weekend doing (1) during one session and then (2) the next training session, in this way you get to ingrain each aspect.

Side stepping is done to throw off the enemy's aim and allow you to engage fast and accurately, as you would hopefully have done thousands of repetitions before being in a real combat situation. This is not a panacea for not getting shot, just a small addition to your overall survival strategy. As you might have noticed in combat video that you will see on the Internet of real-life shootings, it is very hard to shoot a moving target. This is part of your defense when moving. You practice shooting and moving to raise your skill above your opponent's.

When you step, step on the **balls of your feet** smoothly, don't bounce. You will travel about 5 to 10 meters like this, depending on your movement skills. Do this slowly without firing if you don't have the confidence to do it live yet. You will find that it is actually easier to do this faster as you can glide and moving slow does not allow this.

The secret is **smooth movement,** *bouncing* will make it very *difficult to acquire the target* and fire accurately, so make sure the ground is smooth when training initially and watch the target through the sight and soon you will be able to acquire the target while moving. The ground won't be smooth in a combat situation, you do what is possible in a situation when in combat and even if you do fall and get up quickly, you can still be effective.

a. Step to the LEFT side once with all the above aspects in place (**shooting with body position**), fire one shot at a time x 20 repetitions. The shot is fired once the student has done the last step.

b. Step to the LEFT side **2 times** with all the above aspects in place to fire a shot x 10 or 20 repetitions.

c. Step to the LEFT side **3 times** with all the above aspects in place to fire a shot x 20 repetitions.

d. Step to the LEFT side **4 times** with all the above aspects in place to fire a shot x 20 repetitions.

In these pictures, the red arrow shows the shooter moving to his right, gliding the feet, bringing his left foot to the black line indicated while his right foot moves further right along the arrow to the second black line:

1. **Combination** drills: as for Basic Level. Advanced students don't have to hit the target while moving, they just need to move after firing then fire when stopping again.

Elite operator drills for aiming

Exercise 3

It is important that the student be in a balanced stance for the movement drills to work properly and be effective. The target is at **20-30 meters** from the operator. You can also apply the intensity principle here and just cut down the time to engage the target keeping the target at 20 meters. Movement is best practiced on its own so that your mind can concentrate on the movement alone. This could take weeks or months to fully master and understand but is well worth the effort and the ability it gives you in combat. If you have ever shot against someone moving while they have the accuracy to shoot you in the head while moving you will know the fear and frustration to fight a superior exponent.

1. **Stance** drills: as for Basic and Advanced.
2. **Weapon alignment** drills: as for Basic and Advanced.
3. **Targeting** drills: as for Basic and Advanced.
4. **Trigger control**: as for Basic and Advanced.
5. **Side stepping** drills: as for Basic and Advanced but instead of single shots, you fire in groups of 5 at the target.
6. **Combination** drills: as for Basic and Advanced except for the Elite operator student, they have to hit the target while moving, a **center body mass** hit. It can be 2-4 shots in succession as would be applicable for real combat as you won't just fire one shot because the person is trying to kill and *you want to see them drop* before you stop shooting. Training should be both **logical** and **applicable** to your needs: are you training for sports shooting or for real combat, if for sports then it doesn't really matter if you make mistakes or miss and speed or pace doesn't really play a role. In real combat both speed and accuracy are equally important and

should be trained till competent for real life scenarios. This means as fast and accurate as you possibly can, as the more capable you are the more chance of survival.

Additional exercises for elite operator

Focus on your aiming as this is not a movement practice but an aiming drill done without smooth movement, which normally requires you to move faster than you think is possible to shoot accurately at. This could apply to moving between hard cover to hard cover and shooting while you move.

    a. Do the above lateral movement drill shooting 2-3 rounds
        i. do magazine change
        ii. shoot 2-3 rounds
        iii. stop and **scan the area** (we cover Scanning in a section later below, so you'll apply your Basic and Advanced training background here i.e., you'll already know how to do scanning)
        iv. Check you haven't dropped any equipment; this will tell you if you are dressed for success or if you have equipment issues under rigorous movement. If you are at an Elite level, you should not be dropping any equipment at this stage
    b. Do the above lateral movement drill with full 360-degree scan
        i. shoot 2-3 rounds
        ii. do **stoppage drill** (you will need to preload the magazine to cause a stoppage)
        iii. shoot 2-3 rounds,
        iv. stop and **scan the area** front, sides and then back
        v. check you haven't dropped any equipment
        vi. You can do a barrier drill, shooting from cover while

doing a magazine change, as you should always try to reload behind cover. While doing another scan as this is also time which you should use to check your area while you change magazines.

Reminder of your scanning sectors (again, these are covered in detail below):

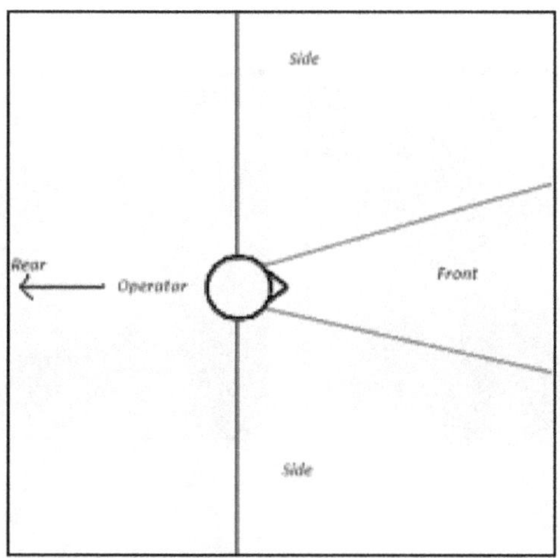

Scanning Technique

Scanning is done **forward <u>and</u> to the sides** before and after a contact. Peripheral vision allows you to see backwards to an extent when turning your head to the side to look.

Scanning with the pistol

Scanning using the rifle

Look, *listen* and *smell* for <u>**target indicators**</u> such as shadows, human shape, barrel protruding, noise (talking/weapons cocking/ scrape of a boot), smell of oil, sweat and fumes, any movement could be an enemy soldier /sniper, OP or LP etc. In a military situation you also look for explosives such as anti-personnel mines, which will be hidden or camouflaged and will be hard to see, and close attention should be given to lines across the path (possible tripwire) as well as any metal protruding from the ground.

The scanning activity can be split into the following directions (sectors)

1. **Forward scan:** is when you look to the front (scan in front) after a contact to see if there is any enemy in front of you.

This is about a 30-degree arc in front of you.

2. Then you can use a **peripheral scan** where you use the slight sideways movement of the head and rely on the **peripheral vision** to pick up any movement that might be on the side of you. This covers the rest of the 180 degrees in front of you. This is demonstrated above in the 3 pictures, without exposing your jaw to being punched and you being knocked out. Keep in mind the reason you are looking behind you is because you don't know who or what is going on behind you, this means the person could be directly behind you.

3. Then we have a **rear look** where you physically turn your body to actually look directly behind you to see more clearly what is behind you. This is only once you are sure any attacker is fully incapacitated and no other threats are in front of you or to the sides. In reality in a war zone or combat situation, you will never be fully able to assess all areas due to buildings or bushes that can conceal an enemy combatant.

    a. The rear look has one application with the pistol where you turn your body so it's about 45 degrees and your head turns the rest of the way to see behind. You don't lift your chin above your shoulder because if there is an opponent and they are close enough to strike, it will be easier to ***knock you out*** if ***your chin is up*** (assuming they don't have a better weapon than a punch/impact option).

    b. The other application is more applicable to the rifle, when you turn side on to the contact which is now on your left or right side depending on which way you wanted to turn. This is when you walk a few steps while you change your mag while checking your six then turn to the front again, to either check for enemy or re-engage the enemy. This technique must be balanced with the desire to keep visual contact with the enemy. If cover was available that will stop incoming rounds, then you should choose this cover to do your checking from and to do the magazine changes behind.

It is important to remember that these movement drills are for open terrain when no cover is available.

<u>**Diagram for scanning sectors**</u>

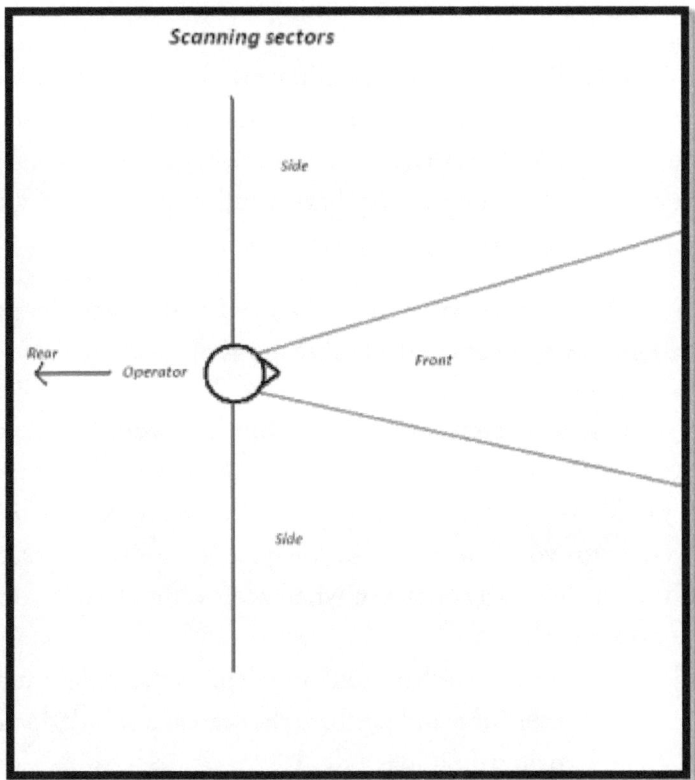

Exercise for scanning

This exercise is to develop or ingrain the student's ability to scan the terrain around them to establish the aspects mentioned when scanning. Basically, it is orientating you to **your team**, the **terrain (cover and concealment, avenues escape and attack)** and **the enemy**. This should be practiced for any operator level (basic, advanced, or expert) as this can be very important to orientation on the battle field. And this will increase your further mental ability as to the next step in your movement and tactics as you get more familiar and the process becomes second nature. This is the reason for all combat training is to get tactics and techniques down becoming second nature.

Initiating the drill: use a whistle to initiate shots for the basic student and use other means such as a shot fired to initiate the commencement of the exercise and let the Advanced and Elite operator students shoot until they are finished, unless they have a full magazine and want to conserve ammunition to prolong the training.

We'll cover the specifics for Basic, Advanced and Expert levels in a moment. First, we go over the drill subsections of the exercise:

- **The initial exercise** is done **standing** and would apply to combat and movement and this would include doing a **low-profile stance** for shooting against the enemy and there is no cover for you. Therefore, the low-profile shooting position is used mostly in a contact or when no cover is close to you to move to.
    - You can either point and depress the trigger and then stop and perform the scan as a simulation or as below do it live.
    - Do live fire 1-3 rounds, stop and do your scan, to keep the process as focused and realistic while

training your accuracy as well as the scanning process.
- ○ Don't just go through the motion, have other students behind to move around and place themselves as you shoot so you can get used to actually looking and seeing what is there. This will be very important in real combat as missing a concealed enemy could be your **last mistake you mistake.**
- Then the above drill is done **kneeling**. This should be done less than any of the other movement techniques. Follow the same system as above for standing:
  - ○ You can either point and depress the trigger and then stop and perform the scan as a simulation or as below do it live.
  - ○ Do live fire 1-3 rounds, stop and do your scan.
  - ○ Have other students behind to move around.
- Then it's done **squatting**. It's faster than kneeling to be able to get up quickly and with less effort unless your backpack weighs 100kg. This will be more practical with a basic combat load of 10-15 kg. Scanning is done after either going through the motions of shooting or actual live fire.
  - ○ You can either point and depress the trigger and then stop and perform the scan as a simulation or as below do it live.
  - ○ Do live fire 1-3 rounds, stop and do your scan.
  - ○ Have other students behind to move around.
- Then it's done **lying** down. It will be harder to scan around without a lot of movement on your part and you may have to sit up to scan properly, which is only possible in a combat situation where there's a lull in firing e.g., if the type of cover allows; if you can roll to better cover and scan from that

position then do that. This is a decision made in combat and will be up to you when and how you do it.

Basic level student

The student stands 10 meters from the target with 5 rounds in the magazine. The target is a full-size target. The student shoots one round and then does the **3 different sectors of scanning** and explains the application of each area scanned. Repeat the exercise till the weapon is empty.

1. The above exercise 5 rounds standing at 10 meters at a target about the size of A4 paper ("Letter" size in the USA). If time allows you can do this exercise with a standing low profile shooting position and a full standing position.
2. The above exercise 5 rounds kneeling at 10 meters size A4.
3. The above exercise 5 rounds lying at 10 meters size A4.

Advanced level student

The student stands 20 meters from the target with 5 rounds in the magazine. The target is a half-size target (this means the normal cardboard target of top half of the body cut in half). The student shoots one round into the target and then does the 3 different areas of scanning and explains the application of each area to scan. Repeat till the weapon is empty.

1. The above exercise 5 rounds standing at 20 meters half size target A4.
2. The above exercise 5 rounds kneeling at 20 meters half size target of the previous target A4.
3. The above exercise 5 rounds lying at 20 meters half size target of the previous target A4. By now the target is very small.

Elite operator level student

The student stands 30 meters from the target with 5 -10 rounds in the magazine, depending on your objectives. The target is a *quarter size* target, by this I mean a normal sized cardboard target cut into 4, using one of the quarters. The student shoots 1-3 rounds (for elite level it must be very accurate) and then does the 3 different areas of scanning and explains the application of each area to scan. Repeat till the weapon is empty. As an added dimension for these operators, you can take some of the magazines and put a dummy round in to simulate a stoppage, this will add a level of calculation and uncertainty which should be easy for an elite level operator to deal with.

1. The above 5 rounds standing at 30 meters quarter size A4 can be done at a low intensity speed initially, but for elite level shooters it ***should get faster*** and even to ***failure to get maximize gains***. This can be done later when you have enough time behind the gun and have the confidence to go at maximum speed. Don't do any maximum intensity drills till you have done 6 months to 1 year of shooting every weekend for at least 2-4 hours.

2. For the 5 rounds kneeling **high profile** stance and then **low-profile kneeling** supported at 30 meters quarter size A4 target, insist that the student takes up the different stances quickly and efficiently without wasted movement or fumbling.

3. For the 5 rounds **lying** in prone at 30 meters quarter size A4 target, you can take a bit more time and focus on your breathing and trigger control but speed is still essential as it's for combat not target shooting.

At this elite level you can work down to a 6x6 inch target (plate if you have them). The student will have to focus to hit such a small target at a range of 30-50 meters (work up to the 50-metre distance) then **scan all three areas**. This will be very demanding and the student can expect to miss some of the time as this is pushing the boundary of accuracy especially when standing up (which will prove to be the hardest).

Peripheral vision

Peripheral vision is the ability to see movement to the side of you when not looking in that direction; this is especially **important in combat** but can be diminished by adrenaline if you don't control your adrenaline rush with the correct mindset and relaxation exercises such as deep breathing.

- One of the drills which helps to combat the effects of adrenaline is the relaxation before or during a contact. During a contact will mean you will need time so it won't be a street surprise mugging. It's more appropriate for an ambush or contact at a reasonable distance. In your mind, tell yourself to physically relax muscles, and breathe deep. This then tells your body to relax as your body associates shallow breathing with stress.
- Scanning also helps to minimize tunnel vision (where you focus on an object in front excluding other things that are going on to your side which your peripheral vision should alert you to).

Exercise 1

This is a non-shooting exercise.

The student stands facing forward and checks at what point another student comes into their peripheral vision. This will show the student where their peripheral vision starts and will give them confidence in peripheral vision.

This can be done 10-20 times then add a shooting exercise to the drill and the student can react and shoot a target in front of them when the person comes into view on either side left or right (or change sides to get some experience with both). This is a more important exercise than most would know as you use your peripheral vision in combat without realizing it.

Exercise 2

This involves reactions to stimulus and quick accuracy training.

The best way to do this is to have targets that can pop up; the student must face side on to the target and react when they see the target move. This is the best way to do this because it's also a peripheral vision exercise to develop your ability to react to movement on the side of you.

The exercise is as follows:

- The student must stand in low ready (see picture below) with the rifle. When they react to the **pop-up target** the student must take up a combat stance, which is bent knees and leaning forward as training like this will give them the combat skills and stance to **deal with recoil** as well as being a more **combat mindset and stance,** higher **mobility potential** and **smaller target** for the enemy. These are the elements of success for combat.
- The target is at:
    - **Basic level** 10 meters, it is also done slower and the student must only concentrate on the exercise, not speed.
    - **Advanced** 20 meters. Here the student can push the speed and accuracy but not maximum or too much intensity, as the person should still be building it up.
    - **Elite** 40-50 meters. This is where maximum speed

and accuracy are expected and should be encouraged, missing or bad safety while handling the weapon means the person is not ready for Elite level shooting.

- Each student will shoot 1 shot at a time with a total of 5 shots and react 5 times to the pop-up target. This is both a peripheral vision exercise and a speed and accuracy exercise, but do not lose your focus on technique because when this breaks down then your combat efficiency will degrade as well.

- Once the 5 shots have been fired, the student must make the weapon safe. Leave the weapon at the shooting line; this is best safety practice, especially if the students are still at a basic level to minimize any accidents. This will not be applied for Elite level shooters as they should have excellent safety by this point. If an Elite level shooter makes any safety violation, then they should also leave their weapon at the shooting line as a disciplinary measure.

Low ready

Exercise 3

Shooting exercise: <u>peripheral vision</u> and reaction time training.

This exercise has the 2 students standing next to each other. The students do not look at each other, it's a peripheral vision exercise so you need to use your peripheral vision and practice it, till it improves and you can easily see and react appropriately.

The student must stand in low ready with the rifle, when they ***react to the other shooter*** the student must take up a ***combat stance*** which is bent knees and leaning forward as training like this will give you the combat skills and stance to deal with recoil as well as more of a *combat mindset.*

The exercise is as follows

- The students can be 5 to 7 meters apart with the target at 5-8 meters
- Although this is a visual exercise, for ***advanced shooters*** you can add:
    - Accuracy at the range they are shooting at
    - Speed at the range they are shooting at, which adds an element of intensity
    - Stress, as this is good for mindset if you do this. Once you lose your mindset you will lose your battle, so maintain the calm focus and deep breathing so you can be combat proficient.
- For more intensity and more of a challenge, the target is next set at
    - Basic level 10 meters
    - Advanced 20 meters
    - Elite 30 - 50 meters

For combat preparedness do this above exercise with movement such as lateral and forward movement, and don't do this without lots of practice. This is the next level up and should be addressed by all who want to be at maximum combat proficiency.

- Each student will shoot total of 5 shots, done 1shot at a time and then the rifle goes back to low ready. The low number of shots is because it's a vision exercise, not accuracy or speed or any other exercise. That doesn't mean you strive for accuracy or speed; your main focus is on your vision.

- For reacting with peripheral vision to the other student, they will change so the total shots that will be fired is 10 shots, once both have fired their rounds, the exercise is over and you can go onto the next exercise. The one student will react to the other shooter and shoot 1 shot at the target and then lower the weapon, this will continue till the 5 shots have been fired. It is irrelevant if the one student shoots all his rounds one at a time till finished. Then the other student fires his rounds. The person moving first could either just do a movement or fire – it's up to you as it's the reacting to this stimulus that's important.

- Once the combined 10 shots have been fired, the student must make the weapon safe, the instructor checks that the weapon is safe and you proceed to the next exercise or start this exercise all over again.

Common scanning mistakes

1. Not checking the sides and back, as some people only check to the immediate sides of the target they just engaged, which is still a frontal-biased direction.
2. Only holding the weapon with one hand. This is a very bad retention position if someone grabs at your weapon from a position of cover such as at a corner of a wall.
3. Lifting your chin up so that any person behind you can knock you out. Do the most secure check you can, don't take a chance that nobody is behind you as they can be very close.
4. Taking your weapon out of line of your area of the main threat, which is directly in front. When looking rearward, your muzzle might drift sideways a bit, but try to keep the weapon pointing as forward as possible. Only move your weapon off a main threat to the front in the event you have

made certain the threat to the front is neutralized or more of a threat materializes from another sector.

5. Not moving laterally when you check to the side and back. Lateral movement is to make you a hard target for someone standing behind you who could be a possible opponent.

6. Omitting scanning in all the basic movement and techniques to save range time. At an Elite level you want to increase the amount of training of your awareness.

Equipment Access

With all combat environments, you should be occupied with **scanning** (deliberate looking with intent and calculation) for the enemy, not looking down at your equipment. This does not mean you never look down at your equipment but you want to minimize this habit especially when in a contact situation.

As much as possible, all weapon control systems must be close to hand such as safety, magazine release, if appropriate slide release controls. The trigger must be comfortable to manipulate as well as the cocking handle. This is because in combat you don't want anything making your task harder than it should be to change magazines and keep firing.

Access without looking

1. Your magazines, including changing magazines
2. Pistol
3. Blade
4. Grenade (if you are a soldier)
5. Radio PTT (push to talk switch)
6. Cable ties
7. Clear stoppage initially by just racking and if needed then assessing (briefly) and then clearing without looking
    a. In the case of a bullet stuck in the barrel you will need to use your pistol to engage the enemy, then clear the obstruction from the barrel.
    b. Most other stoppages clear by tapping the magazine and cocking/racking the weapon.

Exercise

The reason for this exercise is to get the operator used to where the equipment is and being able to access the equipment without looking at it. Do this until it is second nature and then carry on with the next exercise, or do these as part of a series of exercises.

Exercises are to ingrain where the equipment is on your body and how to efficiently access them. Ideally, you want to shoot and then access the equipment as a given magazine becomes empty, so that it is a more natural movement; this applies to all the equipment on your person.

- First do this exercise with dry fire.
- Then do with live fire at a slow pace with focus on smoothness.
- After many hundreds of repetitions can you introduce intensity:
    - The first hundred should be slow and deliberate
    - Intensity can be fast at a pace still controllable
    - Then at a pace where you almost lose control
    - Then at a fast pace while moving, you should be very familiar with the movement and equipment by this time.

1. Operator stands with all equipment ready to shoot and apply tactics and access equipment as is needed, or as the instructor calls out (this will add an uncertain element to the exercise as the operator won't know which piece of equipment the instructor will call out which is exactly what you need in a combat environment as you won't know what the enemy's movement will dictate the need for what equipment).
2. This could be
    a. Change magazines

b. Transition to pistol

c. Access blade

d. Call on radio (only grab radio, you do not need to call in the exercise)

e. Do transition drill if your pistol is on the right otherwise just draw pistol if it's on your left.

f. Access cable ties.

Magazine changes

Once your magazine has run out of ammunition, the normal way to do a magazine change is to use your support hand (left hand for most people) to remove the magazine from the weapon, and then take a mag out of the magazine holder, then to put the next magazine into the weapon. Pick up the half full mag once the fresh mag is in the weapon and stow your half full magazine e.g., in a drop pouch.

It is not always possible in real situations where your focus is on killing the enemy to count the rounds you fired then change a magazine as it runs empty. It is more practical in a long-range engagement to take a magazine out ready to replace the empty one, especially as time is not so pressing in a longer-range engagement such as 150 to 300 meters and where you have the presence of mind.

It is important to remember that when changing a magazine or doing a stoppage drill, what is ***the context*** that you find yourself in and this decides whether it is better to do the following or not

1. **Lower your profile** if no cover is available:

    a. In the traditional special forces (SF) training, this would be done by kneeling; this is if you don't have the necessary movement skills. Movement would be better as this makes it harder to engage you, and moving in a low-profile position would be even better (kneeling is a classic SF move but not the best way to do it).

  b. Leaning forward to make a ***smaller target*** (we prefer this one), this already makes it harder (maybe 5% increase in your survival) to engage you. Now if you add ***movement*** then it's harder still and if you add ***volume of counter fire*** then it's quite effective to engage an enemy with this overall strategy. Your survival can increase by 10-15% (that is just an estimate as nobody knows the actual value in a dynamic real-life situation).

  c. Lying down and shoot roll, shoot roll, etc. This would be good if the attackers are at a good distance roughly 100-300 meters.

2. **Take cover** if cover is available (recall that "cover" is an object robust enough to prevent bullet penetration from reaching you, whereas "concealment" merely hides you perhaps partially, but you can still be shot).

3. **Move**, which is an effective alternative to physical cover. This should be laterally or diagonally towards the enemy if this is applicable for the situation e.g., when entering a cover position.

4. Call "magazine change" (this is if you are in a team) so that one of your team mates can cover you. This won't be needed if you are behind cover. Sometimes you might be covering a specific shooting angle then you might want a fellow operator to cover your angle when changing magazines.

5. Have a magazine in hand while using the right hand to stabilize your weapon then do a speed change.

Position of weapon so you can see the weapon and the enemy. This allows your peripheral vision to work for you to find the magazine well:

Additional contextual aspects to consider:

1. ***Aim for smooth or fluid movement. The operator must not look at the weapon but at the enemy. Know where your equipment is.*** Another important point to keep in mind is to focus on your aiming straight after changing magazines. Shooters tend to neglect the aiming and then pull off a shot wildly. Staying focused will correct this as you will automatically do what you have trained to do in a real situation if the training has been consistent and focused enough.

2. If the context is right, call to your buddy "magazine change" so they can realize your arc is not covered, this will be very

relevant to one operator that is covering the back/rear. *This may not be a good idea if the bad guys are on the other side of your cover position* and you are only 2 operators defending your position, as this will tell the enemy you are not prepared for an assault on your position. Consider before you call magazine change, as this will not even be necessary if you are on your own.

3. **Keep looking at the enemy** and **move to cover if you can** or lay flat if you are far enough from the enemy. If **no cover is available** and there is no time to **lie down** then you should **keep moving**. Keep your eye on the enemy as you want to know if they move, because if they can move and not be seen, this might give them a chance to outflank you.

4. Keep the weapon faced at the enemy when doing your magazine change or pull it in whichever you find is easier for you to do and comfortable to control the weapon while changing the magazine. This will depend on your training, strength and experience. Each person is different with different skills, abilities and capacity to learn so I always allow them to choose which type or way of magazine change they want to use, *it must just be efficient* and smooth.

High-capacity magazines

Keep in mind, especially for an advanced operator, it would be both logical and advantageous to look into using drum magazines that allow you to engage the enemy for up 75 rounds up to 100 rounds. This would be the equivalent of 2 magazine changes of normal 30 round magazines. This will heat up the weapon more as the rate of fire will be sustained and intense due to the tension caused by combat and the person's mindset which is to engaged and neutralize the enemy. The secret is to try to *control the tendency to shoot too fast and uncontrolled* and to focus on short bursts that are well aimed that will actually stop the enemy, instead of firing wildly.

The psychological problems for the operator that they have to overcome can now be to shoot too fast, and too many bullets at a time because of the increase amount of ammunition at their disposal. This can be a subconscious thought pattern because your mind understands that you have more available and you see the enemy and they are shooting at you and your subconscious wants to neutralize the threat.

The positive aspects of hi-capacity magazines

1. Volume of fire
2. Need to change magazines less frequently, this is important in a fire and movement situation
3. Keep the heads of the enemy down longer
4. An assault is less likely to have to stall to reload if your fire discipline is good. For an assault such as getting to a trench and then clearing it, ideally you would want to put on a fresh magazine as the trench will be filled with the enemy.
5. Even though the magazine is heavy and bulky, they are good for an initial contact so balancing standard magazine with high-capacity drum magazine.
6. They are good to carry in your main bag to resupply your ammunition so keeping a spare in the main bag is a good idea (keep in mind it will be very heavy).

Negatives:

1. They can be less reliable than standard magazines
2. The weapon will heat up if fire discipline is not applied
3. Each magazine is heavier and bulkier
4. They are harder to carry due to the bulk of the drum

Advanced operator magazine considerations

Other magazine change options for the AK derivative rifles and Sig as well as any other weapon with a similar magazine release:

Use index finger to press the magazine release to drop the mag

1. Use your trigger or longer middle finger to push the release lever while you reach for the next magazine **simultaneously** (this is applicable to Galil and R4 and AK type weapons).
2. You have two options here: you can ***tilt the weapon*** to see if there are ***any stoppages*** such as a double feed (this is pronation (anti clockwise) of the hand depending on which side the port is) a quick flick or twist of the wrist turns the weapon ejector port to your face, then twist quickly back (this is supination) so you can now put the magazine into the magazine well.
3. This technique tends to work very well with the M4 type weapons whose mags come straight out.
4. If the flick doesn't work then you need to drop the barrel down a bit (from the preferred vertical position shown in the above picture) so the mag will fall out. If it doesn't fall out you can use the mag in your left hand to push the magazine that is in the weapon out. This could be due to the locking mechanism of the AK/R4.

Magazine out first (this refers to the fresh magazine not the one in the rifle)

I.e., here you bring the fresh magazine out before you actually need it. Procedure:

1. Shoot the magazine in the gun until it's nearly empty (20 to 25 rounds in 30 round mag), reach down with your support

hand and remove a full magazine from the magazine holder (chest webbing).

2. The firing hand (right hand for most people) keeps the weapon pointed at the enemy, rifle level to the ground. If your pistol grip on the rifle is straight it might be difficult to hold up parallel to the ground.

3. As the magazine runs empty, use the magazine in your support hand to release the empty magazine and replace with the fresh one.

4. This can be done with fairly calm and focused mindset as you are changing the magazine fairly quick and efficiently.

Additional elite operator technique: held magazine

The other option is to hold an extra magazine in your support hand as soon as you start shooting. The only problem is control – you might find it difficult to manipulate the weapon like this.

You need big hands for this technique, to control and manipulate the magazine; it will be for a short period during a contact. This is a lot easier with pistol magazines but not always possible with a rifle magazine, depending on its size and shape.

Double magazine configuration

A good "tactical change" can be done with a magazine that's placed on the side of your weapon with a bracket called a "ready magazine" that's used for a speed load or **tactical load** (a load done before assaulting a position or receiving an enemy attack).

- Have a "ready mag" bracket on your weapon, as these speeds up the change due to proximity of the spare magazine.
- Or use a double magazine taped together; don't tape them with too much of a gap between the magazines as this can

because the weapon to want to tilt a bit on the side of the spare magazine. (See picture below.)

This picture shows a magazine placed so as not to hinder the safety lever. This can be done by pushing it forward or placing it wider away from the safety. These factors are dictated by the layout of the weapon, especially where the safety is located. Having the second magazine too far out will cause the weapon to tilt on that side, so I keep them as close as possible:

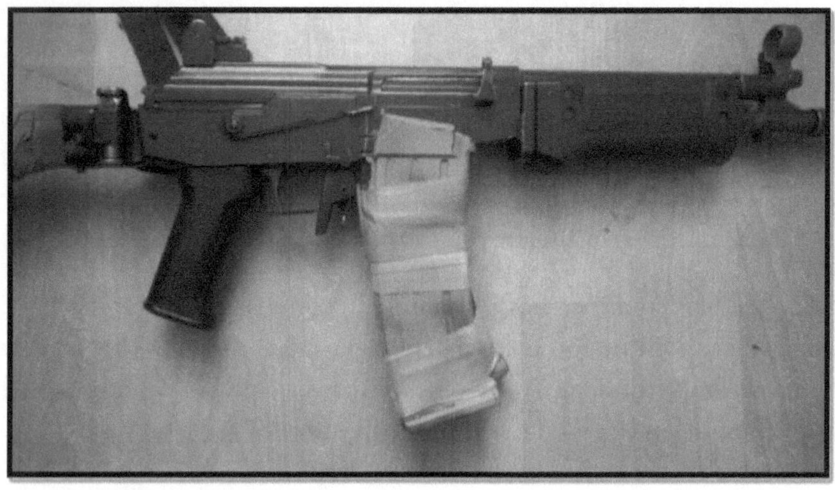

Top view of double magazine shows how close the magazine is to the body of the weapon. It must not prevent the safety from being engaged:

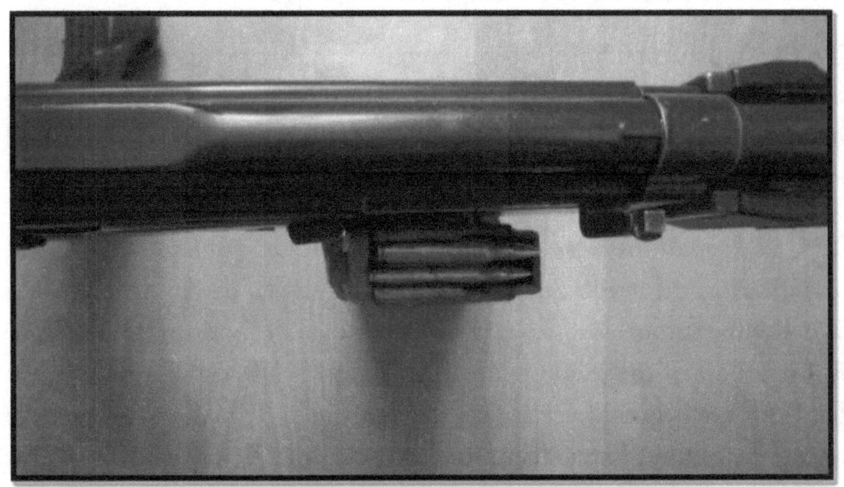

Exercise Drills

How the exercises are applied:

1. Do repetitions of dry drills before doing live fire. **Do not look at the magazine** or **weapon, if possible,** this might feel strange and you will find yourself looking at the weapon instinctively. If so, then try to cut down the time you observe the weapon to a quick glance.
2. Look for the enemy, use your peripheral vision. Do about 20 to 40 repetitions dry fire each day for a couple of days to get the muscle memory. Doing 20-40 a day for a month will make a big difference in the smooth magazine changes.
3. Place target at 30 meters; put 2 rounds in the magazine, person shoots till runs empty, they then do the magazine change. Do about 20 to 40 repetitions; this depends on the amount of ammo and time available.

Exercise 1: Standard magazine change

Do the standard technique for a magazine change i.e., use your support hand to extricate and drop magazine from the weapon then draw out new full magazine from the chest webbing with support hand and place it in the weapon.

This is a ***good time to practice your sight alignment*** and ***target acquisition*** and if you are advanced enough then do the whole thing as a flowing smooth drill to improve your overall shooting ability. That is if it is part of the exercise, fire 1 or 2 rounds otherwise it will be dry fire. Dry fire is good for the first few months so that the main focus is on the magazine change technique, the overall efficiency of the drill is important in the initial phase of the training.

Exercise 2: Index finger drop

For advanced level only.

This is where you simultaneously use your index or middle finger of firing hand to release magazine catch and with support hand take out a new magazine from the webbing/magazine holder. This might only be applicable to weapon systems with the release just below the trigger guard or close enough to use your firing hand:

Advanced shooters should move laterally as you can't give any covering fire if you are on your own, so your only other option is to make yourself a hard target.

Exercise 3: magazine out first

For advanced level only.

This is where you shoot till you have shot out 20 to 25 rounds out of your 30 to 35 round magazines (only put 30-32 rounds in a 35 round magazine so it functions more reliably) then as you've fired about 20 rounds you can reach for the magazine in the webbing and bring it up, holding the weapon with the firing hand and magazine with support hand at the same time. To cut down on training cost, do it with only

5-10 rounds in the mag and count 2-3 shots fired and go for the next magazine in the webbing.

Do what you feel is most efficient for you as an operator, as you will be the one in the fight and you will know what is best for you and your skill level.

You will continue firing till empty. When you hear the click signaling an empty weapon, you use the magazine in your support hand to push the release catch on the weapon and replace the empty magazine with the new one, rack the cocking handle and continue firing if needed.

Exercise 4: magazine in hand

For Elite level only.

Magazine always in hand. This is not as important if you have a double mag on already or you have a ready magazine holder on the side of the weapon.

This is where you take a magazine out of your webbing as soon as it's tactically possible and hold the magazine in your hand as well as manipulate the weapon with the support hand that has a magazine in it.

Once your current magazine runs dry, take the magazine that was in your weapon and replace it with the fresh magazine and, when possible, take yet another magazine out ready to replace the next empty magazine.

Exercise 5: tactical magazine change

All student levels.

This is done when entering a house/enemy bunker, or any scenario where a full magazine is preferable to a half empty magazine. Do this by taking out the half full magazine that is in the weapon and put it into your dump pouch or drop it down your shirt etc., then take a full magazine from the webbing and put it in the weapon. The weapon should still have "one round up" if you had just been shooting and replaced a half full magazine.

Stoppage Clearances

The operator needs to be able to clear weapon malfunctions where a case is stuck in the chamber or in the ejection port (a so called "stove pipe" jam) etc.

Remedial actions

Initial action sequence:

1. Weapon systems stops firing
2. Tap bottom of the magazine
3. Rack the cocking handle to eject any offending cartridge
4. Resume firing.

If above sequence doesn't work, additional steps are required to clear the malfunction:

1. Lift weapon up, don't look down
2. ***For advanced operators turn side on and walk while doing stoppage, you will still need to glance to the front***
3. Look ***through (around) weapon*** so as to be to look forward and see any enemy
4. Remove the current magazine
5. Rack cocking handle, you should see empty case leaving the weapon
6. Put in fresh magazine i.e., unless you are sure the current magazine wasn't causing the malfunction (perhaps it has a weak internal spring), it's risky to return that same magazine to the weapon.
7. Use cocking handle of weapon to charge the weapon again
8. Align body and weapon to target and acquire target through

sights/scope
9. Fire

The above procedure should work for the following stoppage types (see pictures below)

1. Empty magazine
2. Magazine improperly placed on weapon (not seated properly)
3. Fail to fire (dud round)
4. Double feed

Firing (weapon stops) check for cause remove magazine drop or put into pouch

Check (or rack weapon) replace magazine

Rack weapon aim and fire

Types of stoppage

1. Empty magazine
2. Magazine improperly placed in weapon (not seated properly)
3. Fail to fire (dud round)
4. Double feed
5. Case stuck in chamber. You might have to put the stock of the weapon on the ground and stand on the cocking handle to eject a stubborn case (second hardest stoppage to fix in the field).
6. Bullet stuck in barrel (**this is the hardest to fix** and time consuming)
    a. This will require a cleaning rod to tap the bullet out with, this normally takes quite a few taps on the bullet as it is quite tight in the barrel, normally the kinetic energy is used to push the bullet out.
    b. It is time consuming so you will need to find cover to apply this.

Standard stoppage clearance procedure

Technique (the first 3 take place **simultaneously if it's ingrained through training**):

1. **<u>Don't look down</u>** at the weapon, **look forward** through the weapon. If you need to assess what the problem is, use a quick glance to assess and then look forward. Doing this will develop a habit of looking to the enemy instead of concentrating on the weapon in your hand. Prefer looking forward if the stoppage is not too complicated.
2. Call to your buddy "stoppage" **<u>if the context is correct</u>**, that is **if there are a number of you and you are not too close to the enemy such as in a room next door**, he will cover your arc for you. If you are fighting on your own then moving and assessing is best and most expedient, you might also be looking for cover now if you were not in cover already.
3. Keep weapon faced at the enemy, you can also tilt it to see in to assess the type of stoppage. This allows a better view of the ejection port and chamber of the weapon once the cocking handle is pulled back.
4. Take cover if possible.
5. Move to the side and crouch or **continue moving if in the open**, be careful of your buddy's arc of fire when in a team. For individual combatants on their own this will not be a problem.
6. Crouch low, keep a low profile use 2 second gaps to look sideways at where your teammates are. If you can do a 30 degree to the front and a 180-degree scan to sides if the fight has slowed down then do so. *Situational awareness* is very important in a battle.
7. **Tap** the bottom of the magazine and pull **the cocking handle** back. If you can see that there is no stoppage from

malfunction then the magazine was empty or the magazine was not seated properly, then release to feed round in.

    a. If the magazine is empty, change it. Normally your mind will have calculated that if you have shot for a certain number of shots you assumed at the magazine is empty, from training your mind can subconsciously count and keep a rough tally of shots fired.

    b. If you can see that there are cases stuck in the chamber then release the magazine. On the AK, Galil and R4 you can do this with your support hand, rack the cocking handle **twice** or three times, your support hand reaches for the full magazine.

    c. If you see a double feed, release the magazine, rack twice, place new magazine in and cock the weapon.

8. Aim and fire, for close in point aim.

9. If you have a case stuck in the chamber and it won't come out, you may need to push it out with a rod, especially if the rim for the extractor is damaged. Tape a rod to your weapon if you are unfortunate enough to have a weapon that has this type of stoppage often. It may be a good idea to get another weapon if this is a regular occurrence.

Exercise drills for Basic and Advanced level

The stoppage drill is combined with intermediate distance to add an aiming aspect to the drill as it's expedient to try to use the ammunition expeditiously. To add an advanced flavor to this exercise, add some movement to it. The primary goal is a stoppage drill so focus is on this aspect but to use the ammunition correctly as you will be shooting live ammunition. Don't do the movement part if it's a novice shooter but for advanced shooters it will be expected for them to apply all aspects of good shooting form.

Layout of range

Put 1 to 3 targets at about 10 meters for basic student and 30 m for advanced student. Place 1 or 2 live rounds in the magazine then an empty shell then another 2 live rounds. The student must engage the target effectively and clear the stoppage in one smooth movement without looking at the weapon.

Exercise 1: magazine change drill

Put 3-5 rounds in each magazine, have at least 6 -7 in the magazine in the rifle and 6 in your chest webbing.

1. Stand with magazine in rifle at high ready, with full chest rig
2. Use any initiating sound to start the drill: shout, whistle, gunshot etc.
3. Engage each target till magazine empty, focus on accuracy, when you run empty change magazine with a smooth fluid movement:
    a. Basic shooter takes their time
    b. Advanced shooter adds a time constraint
    c. For Elite level shooter, time constraint and with movement.

For this empty magazine scenario, just replace that magazine. Use the slide lock on your weapon if it has one. On the AK derivative weapon systems which do not go to slide lock if the magazine is empty, you will still need to do a racking (cocking) motion to charge the weapon.

Exercise 2: simulated stoppage

A simulated stoppage drill can be done by letting the student stand in stance with weapon aimed; the drill can commence when instructor calls "stoppage!", or use live fire with a dummy round loaded at a random level in the magazine by the instructor to cause a stoppage.

<u>Basic student level</u>

On experienced the stoppage, tap the magazine and rack the cocking handle, proceed to fire slow and deliberate, so you don't waste ammunition and can train accuracy as well.

If the weapon does not fire, hold back the cocking handle and tilt the rifle barrel up, twist the hand palm down (this is called pronation) as you look at the possible problem while still being able to look forward to see the enemy approaching. Clear the type of stoppage you see and proceed shooting. This should be done as quickly as possible once the person has a good idea of how it is done effectively. But as with all techniques it must be done slowly at first to learn the subtleties.

<u>Advanced level</u>

Rack and fire immediately after the slide stops moving, the focus of this drill is to react quickly to the weapon stopping, and smoothly rack without hesitation to clear a stoppage. If the rifle clicks again (magazine empty) then a fresh magazine can be placed in the weapon. As the instructor you should monitor the student's mindset and tension levels as much as possible and correct any tension showing on their face. This is especially pertinent for advanced level shooters.

If the weapon does not fire, hold back the cocking handle and tilt the rifle barrel up as you look at the possible problem while still being able to look forward to see the enemy approaching. Clear the type of stoppage you see and proceed shooting, deliberately and focusing on accuracy.

Exercise 3: unseated magazine or dud round

Because you won't know if it was an unseated magazine or if it is a dud round you will normally just *tap the magazine* and *rack the cocking handle*. This is considered a standard drill for any type stoppage in a semi auto rifle. That's why this stoppage drill is called the "Tap rack" drill.

Exercise 4: feed failure

Remove the magazine that is in the weapon and rack the cocking handle a few times, normally once or twice will do the trick. Put the magazine back in after any round that failed to feed has fallen clear out the ejector port, or replace that magazine with a fresh magazine, proceed to fire.

Advanced and Elite level operator stoppage drill

This can be done as follows, each drill becoming more intense:

1. 10-50 times slowly, **no live** fire, to understand the drill, familiarize yourself with the weapon magazines and magazine carrying method, the webbing. The more drills you do now, the easier the process becomes later on.
2. 10-20 times **slowly live** fire, focus on a smooth drill and try not to look at the equipment unless it's a quick glance.
3. 10 faster **live fire.**
4. Maximum intensity if the student is at a high enough level to apply this, do these 5 to 10 times.

Range layout for the drill:

1. Place 2 or 3 targets at 3-8 meters (if the person is advanced then place them 10 meters) so that the focus is on the stoppage drill and not on the aiming and shooting aspect.
2. The targets can be 2 to 4 meters apart.

This drill utilizes **point aim** with the assault rifle/carbine:

1. The student will shoot 1 to 3 rounds
2. Then encounter a dud/dummy round used to cause the stoppage, loaded by the instructor
3. Tilt the weapon to see the ejection, for the following reasons:
    a. To **asses** stoppage
    b. **Position** weapon for point aim
    c. Pull the **cocking** handle backwards (on LM/R4/ Galil type weapons)
    d. Because it is open over the top, and not restricted by the sights, the operator can **see more clearly** for close range encounters
    e. Release the handle and fire immediately 1-3 shots in point aim position at 2 to 3 targets.
    f. Assess your surroundings: 30 degrees, then 180 degrees, then behind.
    g. Focus on smooth, not fast.

Use this range layout if you want an additional stress factor to the above stoppage drill:

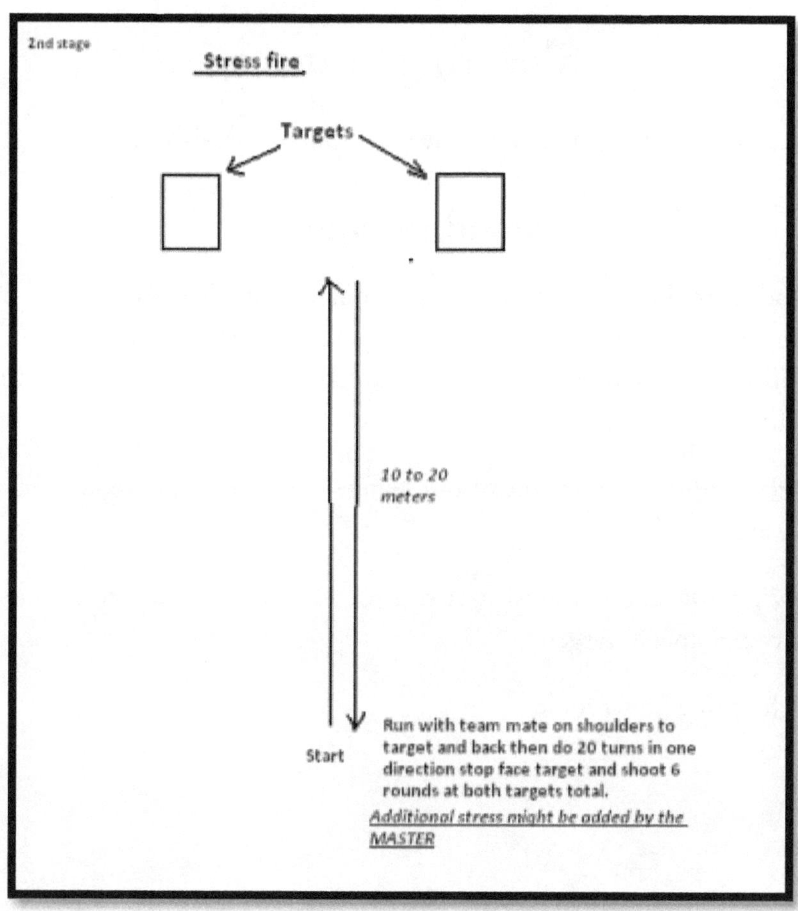
2nd stage
Stress fire
Targets
10 to 20
meters
Start
Run with team mate on shoulders to
target and back then do 20 turns in one
direction stop face target and shoot 6
rounds at both targets total.
Additional stress might be added by the
MASTER

Shooting Stances

These shooting positions are done in the open, not with a cover barrier.

Standing stance

Stand with knees bent, lean approximately 20 degrees forward to compensate for recoil, but the person must still try to remain in balance to allow further movement in any direction. There are two standing positions you can take:

High profile standing position: where you are only slightly bent forward.

Low profile standing position: you are in a very low stance to make yourself a smaller target.

High profile Low profile

Shooting in different directions

This applies to minimal movement and more about turning the body, but sometimes requires small movement with your feet when standing and knees when kneeling.

These exercises are to develop your ability to turn on the spot and not moving in any specific direction.

It is important to remember that when shooting in different direction with your rifle you should have a good shooting stance that is **balanced** and controlled that means you can move in any direction with ease.

Standing on one spot

Finger off trigger

1. **Shooting forward**: is basically just lifting the rifle to a point aim position for close range targets (0 - 20 meters or a little further depending on level and program goals). For aiming at targets out to 50 and further, you will need to take your time and make sure of the sights. This would change the exercise from a pointing exercise to an aiming one, the basic stance and body position is still exactly the same, when doing the point aim for medium to long range or using your sights.

2. **Shooting left and right**: requires turning your torso but if you are not flexible in this regard then move your feet till you are able to shoot to the side, this shouldn't take much movement of the feet. If you want to point left, moving the right foot a few inches forward should accomplish this and it's the opposite for the other direction.

3. **Shooting backward**: you can't pull the weapon in like a pistol, to prevent someone grabbing it, and you can't really shoot with one arm like you can with a pistol, you therefore should **step forward** and **to the side**, then turn. This does two things: gets you out of range of any person approaching from behind i.e., creates space, and moving to the side takes you out of line of incoming rounds.

    ◦   Turning to shoot backward to the left is possible but you won't have the stable shooting platform if you don't also move your feet. Because this is a stationary drill you therefore will stay in place and turn to maximum and then stop and shoot.

    ◦   Turning to shoot backward to the right is possible to a lesser degree due to the limited movement of the spine and you would therefore have to move your feet. It's also easier for an attacker to grab the barrel as it's fractionally closer to the attacker.

Do not obscure your peripheral vision:

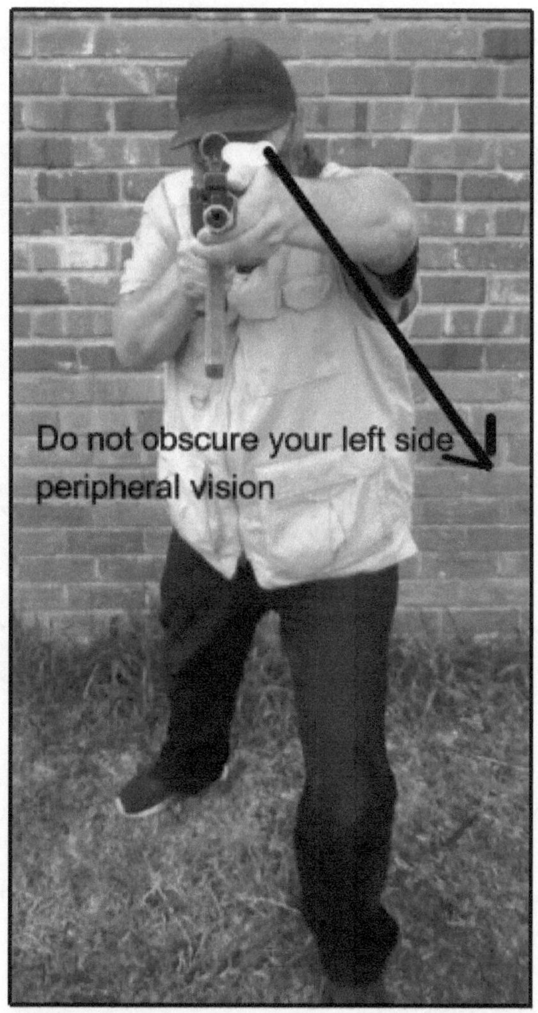

This is how you might obscure your left side peripheral vision on the left side:

Kneeling stance

A kneeling position facing forward allows for rotating to the rear to engage/scan, and turning back to facing forward again, bringing the knee that is up towards the other knee that is down and lifting the knee that was down to the upright position to do this.

There are various options:

<u>The high kneel</u>: the weapon is not supported on the leg (knee area against the elbow). This might be due to an obstacle that does not allow the shooter to go into a supported kneeling position.

<u>The low kneel</u>: you sit on the rear heal, when you have time and the shot requires a more stable platform to shoot from. This is where the shooter will be in a lower position and their elbow will be placed on the knee, but be slightly over so the meaty part of the triceps is on the knee and not the bony part of the elbow.

<u>Low kneeling with low profile</u>: lean forward a lot more than normal

<u>Kneeling with both knees on the ground</u>.

<u>Squatting position</u>: you sit on your heels not putting your knees down. This is for low cover and is very fast to get up from, thus a good stance for quick movement up and down where a quick stop is needed before going on. Notice the closer the rifle is to your centerline, the easier it is to move and balance. This will be an unstable stance in a front-back direction so if you shoot multiple shots in a row, especially a heavier caliber weapon, it might push you over, unless you weigh 100kg or more:

The fastest way to stay mobile is to use a low-profile stance instead of a kneeling position, especially if running and shooting (fire and movement or outflanking). The stance as shown below allows you to move fast and get down and up again with very little time in between:

Kneeling shooting technique

Facing forward: left arm can either **float** for quick shots or **rest** with the triceps on the knee not the point of the elbow bone (ulna) on the knee. This would be called low kneeling supported.

Shooting left and right: is restricted because of the torso that can only turn a restricted distance. Here you might need to turn the hip by putting down your left leg if you want to turn to the right and don't have the flexibility in your spine. This is demonstrated below and as can be seen *dropping either the left or right* knee so that the two come together to allow the muscles of the external rotators in the glutei maximus to stretch and then contract forcefully to allow fast efficient movement in the opposite direction. This allows you to turn

180 degrees very fast and smoothly when applying this technique (see below)

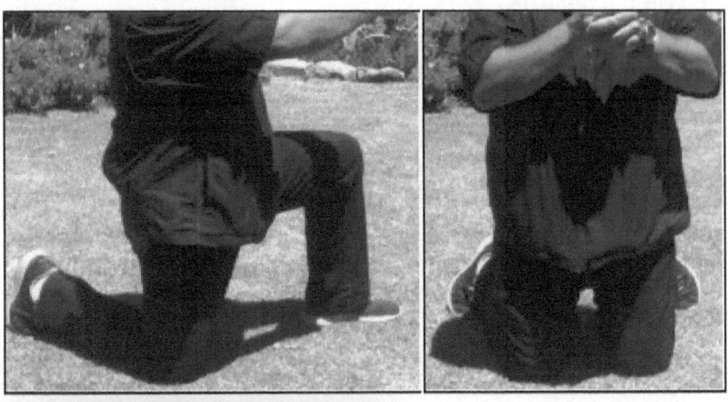

You only need to turn your upper body to acquire the target on your left side; this is facilitated by the flexibility of the spine and minimal leg movement.

Shooting backward: Because you can't pull the weapon in to prevent someone grabbing it, move forward, this means you might need to **get up** and step forward and then turn to the side. This is a bit slow and that's the reason I prefer to use a low-profile stance than going into a kneeling stance because of the <u>mobility issues</u>.

Otherwise turning to your left is fairly easy, you can turn to face backwards if you put your knee down then lift the alternate knee and this will face you backwards.

Turning right you need to drop the left knee and bring up the right knee.

High kneeling (unsupported): Low kneeling (supported):

Lying down

The basic lying position should be comfortable so that your breathing does not affect your aim. Some suggest pulling your one leg up to allow the diaphragm to move easily but *if you are fit* this should not make such a difference. The arms will be under the rifle for support if this position is applicable to your context, which is a higher profile shooting position.

You'll be shooting in 3 different directions:

Forwards, lying on your stomach

Shooting to the front is the normal shooting position you apply most times:

Sideways, left and right, lying on your side

Shooting to your left and right means leaning on your side, which is more uncomfortable; lean on your right shoulder if you are a right-hand shooter. Lying down on your side is used to shoot below a low obstacle, which could be a fence, vehicle, or some other obstacle. If transitioning from stomach/back, you will need to roll onto your side and use your legs to balance your body and or assist with the movement.

Backwards, lying on your back

Shooting to your front when on your back means lifting your head and upper body up if on a flat surface. When shooting close, use your barrel as an aiming point of reference for your eyes and brain.

To shoot behind, you either have to lift the rifle over your head or turn onto your stomach.

Crawling forward

High crawl and low crawl, weapon facing forward is used in all tactical situations by snipers and infantry soldiers where the cover does not allow an upright movement.

In one of the low crawl techniques taught to soldiers, they suggest the weapon be dragged along on one side of your body just over the arm, normally the right arm. I would **not suggest** you do this because the weapon is not available fast enough and you can be caught off guard and possibly get shot without even being able to fire a shot off. You should at least have a suppressed pistol in your hand if you are going to crawl with your rifle (sniper) behind you.

Rolling can be used to get to cover while making you a lesser target. Rolling is used when going from low cover to low cover, in both urban and bush warfare.

Lying down shooting technique

It is important to have a comfortable position, which is not always possible in real combat but when available take one. Relaxed posture is important so that when you pull the trigger it can done with a certain amount of relaxation and control and this is achieved with deep breathing. As can be seen below the *arms are at about 45 degree pointing at the centerline* balancing out, this should be comfortable and put no strain on your neck or other muscles holding the weapon up. As you can see in the picture, the force vectors will cancel each other out and it should take no effort to keep the weapon in a stable position for a long time. If you have elbow pads you should be able to stay in the position for an extended period of time. Now that you have a stable relaxed position to shoot from you can concentrate on the trigger control of slow tension till the trigger breaks.

For combat rifle, breathing into the stomach will help with minimizing movement, and having adequate oxygen is important if you need to run. Breathing is going to affect your aim slightly in combat but not enough to worry about it. Breathing into the lower stomach helps to not move the whole upper chest cavity either up or down. This also allows more air to be breathed in than with chest breathing, which means you can be more relaxed.

As with all quick and accurate shooting it is important to get used to shooting *when you are on target – don't wait*, pull that trigger (you would have done target ID). This has to be practiced otherwise you won't be able to do it in reality. This is as much a technique as it is a mental exercise, because people tend to not shoot immediately because they feel they might not be on target, so it needs confidence. The secret is don't expect a 100 percent perfect target and sight picture.

Pull the trigger straight back and don't pull in a jerky motion, let the shot go and wait a split second, this is called "follow through", then find your target again as the recoil would have taken you off the target. Apply this sequence if time and situation allow this type of shooting under control. If you have multiple enemy targets then your priority is engaging as many as possible with effective fire.

45-degree
angles for arms

Lying down side view

On your stomach, to maintain control of the rifle, you will normally have to keep both hands on the weapon to hold it up and control the recoil. As can be seen above the arms must form an equal and opposite force to form a bipod as this is the best way to have a controlled and stabled platform. This is not always possible in real combat but can be attempted when possible and viable.

On your back, to maintain control of the rifle you will normally have to keep both hands on the weapon to hold it up and control the recoil:

Shooting from a seated position

This could be from a vehicle seat, very seldom in a house with a rifle unless you are on military operation or a farmer in South Africa where they brutally murder and torture farmers because of the color of their skin (typically white, the communist government is complicit in this and it's therefore one of the most dangerous professions in South Africa).

As with all shooting, the position of the weapon or the structure is very important to fast sight and target acquisition. All aspects of aiming apply except for the base of the structure which would be your feet on the ground but in this instance, it will be a seated position. The upper body doesn't change and is therefore easy to shoot as per standing

Barrier Shooting (Using Cover)

This section deals with the stances that are used when shooting from a barrier. The focus is not on how to use the cover itself, as that is dealt with later on. Below see shooting from a berm by operators:

As with all combat situations, it's important to remember the context of the situation will be the deciding factor when you want to apply a **technique/stance** to a situation. Due to the nature of combat and the enemy's intention to incapacitate you, it is usually advisable to expose as little as possible to the enemy and only let the weapon itself stick out:

We'll now cover the various scenarios of using barriers:

Free standing unsupported

Stand about 1 to 2 meters from the barrier and *leaning out*, this is **not tilted** and is quite exposed, so this should only be used for **long range targets** over 50 meters away. Keep in mind an enemy bullet will fly along the wall at about 4-6 inches from the wall and stay at that distance from the wall i.e., it flies parallel to the wall.

When **standing free** but the **target is close** you should *expose as little as possible* and this requires you to lean a lot or **tilt your body** so only the weapon and your eye stick out. (See below).

When standing, **engage one target at a time** progressively repositioning your feet after each target has been engaged so that you can see more around the barrier to the next one. So, for shooting around the ride hand side of a barrier, you engage the targets from right to left, one by one. ***Don't try engaging or see all the targets at once***, as this will expose too much of your body. Training target distances:

1. Basic operator 10 meters
2. Advanced operator 20 meters to the front
3. Elite operator 30 to 50 meters to the front; this will most likely be outside as you won't have many indoor situations where you will use a wall or doorframe as cover at that range. It is more applicable to outside combat such as using the wall of a house.

the wrong
way

Standing supported

This is when the rifle is being braced on the cover by your hand, especially when the target is at more than 50 meters from you. This is a position that could be used more than you might think. The only time you don't tend to use cover is when the enemy is close and you need to move and shoot. Try to brace the weapon so it doesn't contact a hard surface if possible.

1. Basic operator 20 meters
2. Advanced operator 40 meters to the front
3. Elite operator 50 to 100 (increase to 300 meters, increments of 50) meters to the front, place 2 or 3 targets at these ranges so the person can practice holding off for extended ranges as well as the bracing.

Kneeling in low cover

Don't choose a barrier that is not ballistic protection as you might as well run further and get to better cover.

Kneeling supported on your knee or supported on the barrier will be slightly different in their overall application. Supported on the barrier will be more stable and leaning on your knee behind the barrier will be slightly less stable. Kneeling is not ideal if the cover is not high enough.

The distance chosen for the different levels of operator will apply to average population; some nations have a shooting culture and will find these distances easier:

1. Basic operator 20 meters
2. Advanced operator 40 meters to the front
3. Elite operator 50 to 100 meters to the front, place 2 or 3 targets at these ranges

Correct forward lean in high
kneeling

Squatting in low cover

This is when you sit onto your heels without your knees touching the ground. This is a quick stance to take and quick to get up from. This lends itself to fire and movement where you take cover and move frequently. It isn't very stable to shoot from as it is a balancing stance and is hard to shoot multiple shots from. It can be fairly stable if combined with a rifle supporting position as when leaning the rifle on a low wall. It's not an accurate firing position but it's good for movement and shooting:

1. Basic operator 10 meters
2. Advanced operator 20 meters to the front
3. Elite operator 50 meters to the front, place 2 or 3 at these ranges

Prone barrier shooting

Lying down at a barrier requires the operator to lie on their side when shooting to minimize exposure to the attackers. See picture below. It does take getting used to as weapon sight picture is slightly harder to get. It can also be hard to stay in the side position for longer periods.

1. Basic operator 20-40 meters
2. Advanced operator 50-60 meters to the front
3. Elite operator 100 meters to the front, place 2 or 3 targets at these ranges of 60, 80- and 100. It takes good core strength and arm strength as you have to hold the position with your muscles:

Wrong way better way to lie down at a barrier

Two man shooting position

This depends on terrain or make up of the building or cover structures. The place you stand will be dictated by the maximum amount of cover available and your objectives for e.g., entering a building structure. See below:

Correct use of cover

The correct use of cover in a combat situation is essential for you to be able to engage the enemy while not getting shot yourself.

1. Leaning to the side, exposing as little of your body as possible. This needs to be practiced, as when you look at the sights it will be different looking at an angle compared to looking at them vertically, and this can make you miss the target so you

will need a few hours on just shooting tilted to the side at an angle. The other aspect which seems to be difficult is getting the body able to lean and hold that position for a few seconds. That is possibly why many people do not lean out and use cover to its maximum.

2. Look around your cover, low and then high but try never to look over the cover. This is because you highlight yourself above the cover and can expose more than you want to. You will see from pictures of using cover that when going low you should minimize the target area the enemy can shoot at.

3. Come up in a different position each time. This causes the enemy to search for you giving you time to shoot back as they try to see where you came up. This gives you a time period to take aim if you know where they are and can effectively engage them. The time period might only be 1-2 seconds that you have to engage so don't look for tool long as you will give them the opportunity to engage you.

4. Always reload your magazine behind cover, or if no cover is available then kneel to make yourself a smaller target and if the person is far enough from you, you can lie down and roll to change you cover position. If you don't have cover then taking up a low-profile stance can assist but is not a panacea for not getting shot.

5. Do not position too closely to the cover, rather give yourself space to move and so that you are able to look behind you. This is also important as being close to cover means the bullet can ricochet off the cover and hit you. It limits your movement and closes your field of vision. This is more for moving around buildings and when you are in a fixed position you might have less of these problems. For instance, a foxhole gives the defender basically 360 degrees of cover.

6. When engaging multiple targets, start from one side only

engaging one at a time, ensure team members watch the other side and your back. This engaging one at a time from cover, as you use the cover to maximum effect, means you will only see one target at a time. This is in a limited context as won't apply to a foxhole or open terrain where the enemy are spaced out in front and are all visible.

7. When approaching corners, give yourself space so your weapon is not grabbed from the front as you turn a corner and you have reaction time – crucial in combat especially when the enemy is all round you.

8. If lying down, roll to come up somewhere else or to the next solid cover and if you are standing you will have to either crawl or move quickly to cover in a crouch. When the enemy is 100 meters or more away from you then it is reasonable to take a prone position as they have to cover a lot of ground to assault you and this means you can see and engage them.

9. Do not let the weapon protrude from cover, as this will give your position away and tell the person when you are moving out of cover. This is more applicable to moving in and around buildings when moving slow and stealthy. If enemy see the barrel first, they can get ready and engage you at their own time accurately.

10. When searching a house on your own, look around corners low (kneeling) using peripheral vision, pop head in and out then move to the other side and check the other side. It takes time but rather that than getting shot. This is more single operator stealth and movement as in SHTF type scenario, but can also apply to small team operations where stealth and security are at their utmost necessity.

11. You want the enemy to see as little as possible and still be able to engage the enemy:

Exercise: progression drill

Place 3 targets at 5-meter intervals apart in front of the cover, 30 m from the cover. The student must stand away from the cover so they can move and engage each target individually exposing as little of themselves as possible. They must shoot from right to left, and then change from left to right, one bullet per target. As the student becomes more advanced, add in a time constraint starting at 13 seconds going down to 10 sec.

Exercise: barrier drill

Targets are placed behind barriers moving away from the student. The student must move down the line of barriers to engage each target as they see them. Place approximately 5-10 barriers at 5 m apart.

For beginners, use one or two targets. For advanced student, add in time constraint of 10 sec for 2 targets, 12 to 14 sec for 4 targets.

Exercise: Target to target transition drill

Depending on the level of the operator, use 2 to 4 targets that are operated by the instructor to rise up so the student can engage them. This is done as randomly as possible. The student can have a magazine with 10 rounds in and will engage the targets until empty.

1. Basic student targets are at 10 meters using 2 targets that pop up. No time limit the target is lowered when the student shoots. The targets are spaced about 10 meters apart.
2. Advanced student targets are at 30 meters using 3 targets that pop up. There is a 3 second time limit when lifting the target then it must be lowered.
3. Elite operator student targets are at 50 meters using 4 targets that pop up. Because of the range and number of targets they may have to be 5 meters apart. Time limit as for advanced level, or quicker if possible.

Shooting While Moving

Remember: always keep your **finger off the trigger while moving**.

There are various directions of movement and their technical implications:

1. **SWAT walk forward**, heel toe slowly and controlled. This will have been covered in pistol training and needs only to be rehashed for control of the rifle while moving. Picture sequence:

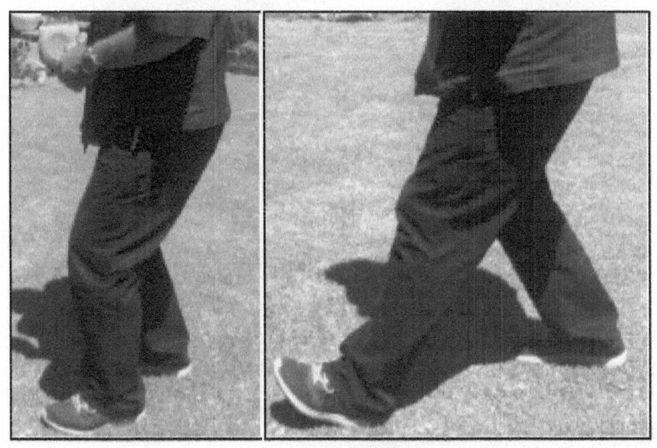

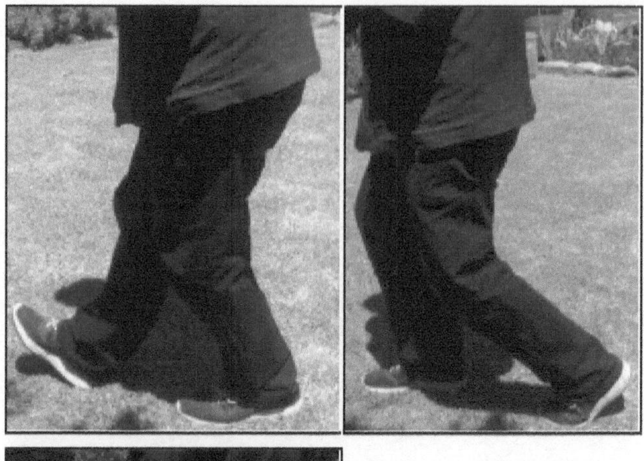

1. **Left and right**: the foot leads that is on the side you are going to so if moving right, you start by moving your right foot. This is lateral movement and for close engagements you move fast and for far engagements move slowly and shoot more deliberately so your long-range accuracy is better.

    a. **Lateral movement** can be either **slow deliberate** side steps to take you out of the line of fire, done 2 or 3 times till you have effectively engaged the target. This is not so easy at longer ranges but it's not going to be easy for the enemy to shoot you either (it's harder for any shooter to engage a moving target than a stationary one).

    b. **Lateral movement** can also be **fast and fluid** to be more of an evading tactic in relatively close quarters but, as with all real combat, the situation (context) dictates the tactic. For example, if solid cover is immediately available then this should be used and if no cover is available then move till the attacker is down and out of the fight.

2. **Backward movement:** to engage enemy while moving backward. This takes a low stance with good balance and an ability to move on the balls of your feet, to make the stance stable and have as little up and down body (and thus rifle) movement as possible. You will need to be careful of falling over objects behind you. Should you fall, it's not a major problem as you can shoot from the ground but can be a problem if you are being attacked by a person with a blade at close range.

3. **Diagonal movement:** is neither moving forward or left or right but at an angle to the target which is both forward and sideways. See diagram below.

Master moving in all the above directions, going into a **kneeling** or **squatting** position, get up and move again and go into a low position, as this will be most conducive to combat type movement and scenarios where you will move and then look and position yourself behind any available cover.

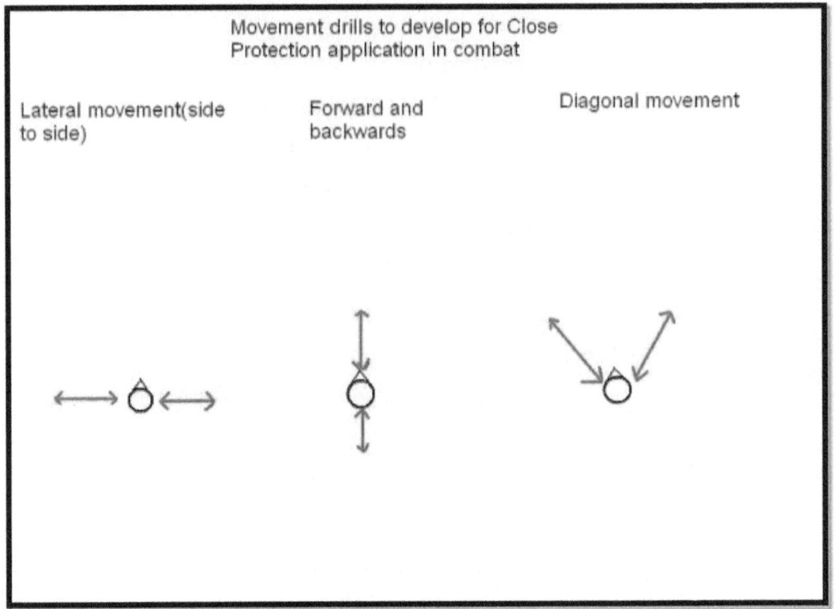

Exercise

The exercise is done 5 times slowly dry fire, then 3-5 times live fire. If possible, make a video recording of the 3rd live fire run so that it is an accurate depiction of the student's current ability. This can be used to show the person's short comings at a later date or immediately, to help them understand and able to correct mistakes.

This should give you a good work out and will deal with most shooting positions:

1. Set up range with targets such as 5 paper and 3 falling plates. There are no hard and fast rules, so change the range layout as needed:

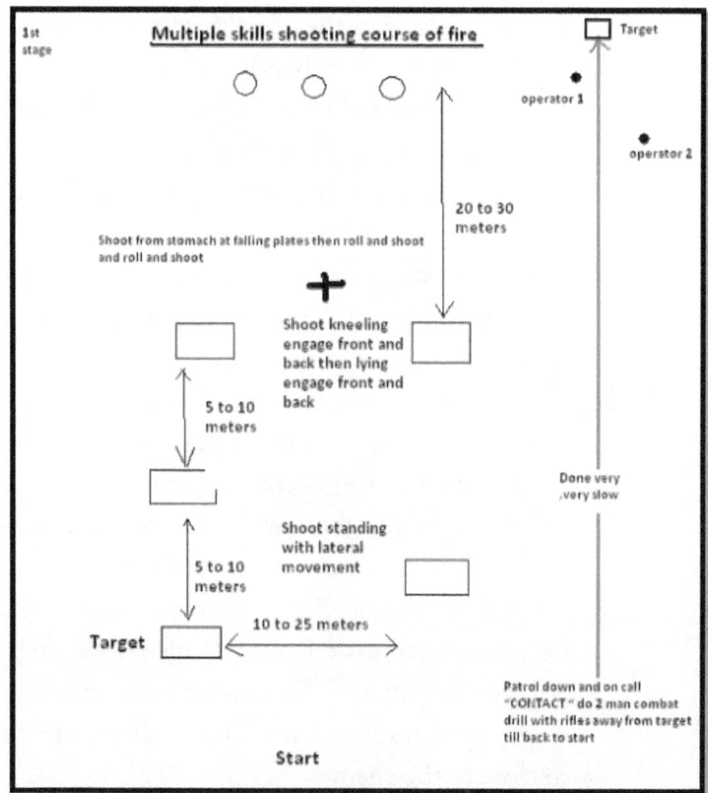

1. The shooter can have a full magazine of 223 caliber rifle or whatever carbine/PDW they are using for the exercise.
2. As dictated on the diagram below, the shooter starts at the start point, either initiated by themselves or by the instructor.
3. Unless otherwise directed, start with the rifle in low ready:
4. You walk forward with weapon in ***low ready*** and as you come in line with the left target, lift the rifle and do a quick turn and shoot, while move laterally if applicable and if possible due to range conditions and safety considerations. You can either walk as in a patrol or as in a SWAT scenario – this will be up to the instructor to decide which situation you will be more likely to find yourself in:

a. For variation, start the exercise with a punch to a small pad to tire your hands out as would be more than likely in certain types of single combat context, so the punching can be either left out or used according to the instructor's needs. It would be even more useful if you know the correct punching technique even if the striking is used for tiring the hands and arms out i.e., don't undermine your striking technique in doing this shooting exercise.

b. For variation, start exercise with a head butt, elbow, or knee strike. This is a good close-range striking combination and a good drill. For this drill you either have to put the rifle down or swing it to your back, but this can be very uncomfortable as the weapon will swing all over the place so it's maybe better to put it down before doing any striking. This is more likely in a SHTF event or in a civilian mugging, as it's rare that soldiers will find themselves so close to the enemy.

5. Continue moving laterally to engage 3rd target. As you move you can either engage till you hit the target or as per instructor's orders e.g., only shoot 2 shots then move on, regardless of whether the shots hit or not.

6. Move laterally to the 4th target and go into kneeling, shoot one or 2 rounds then engage the target behind you ***if this is a safe practice on your range***. Don't do this if it's either unsafe or there is no back stop to catch the round.

7. If you need to change magazines at any point, do so without looking at the magazine or rifle as this should be ingrained by now and should always be part of your training drills.

8. Now go down prone and engage 3 falling plates from the ground, but you must roll then shoot. Change magazines if

needed

Demonstration video

To see this in real time live action go to: Intercept Training Concepts on YouTube. Here are still images from that footage:

Exercise: stress fire

You can expand the above drill into a second stage for stress fire:

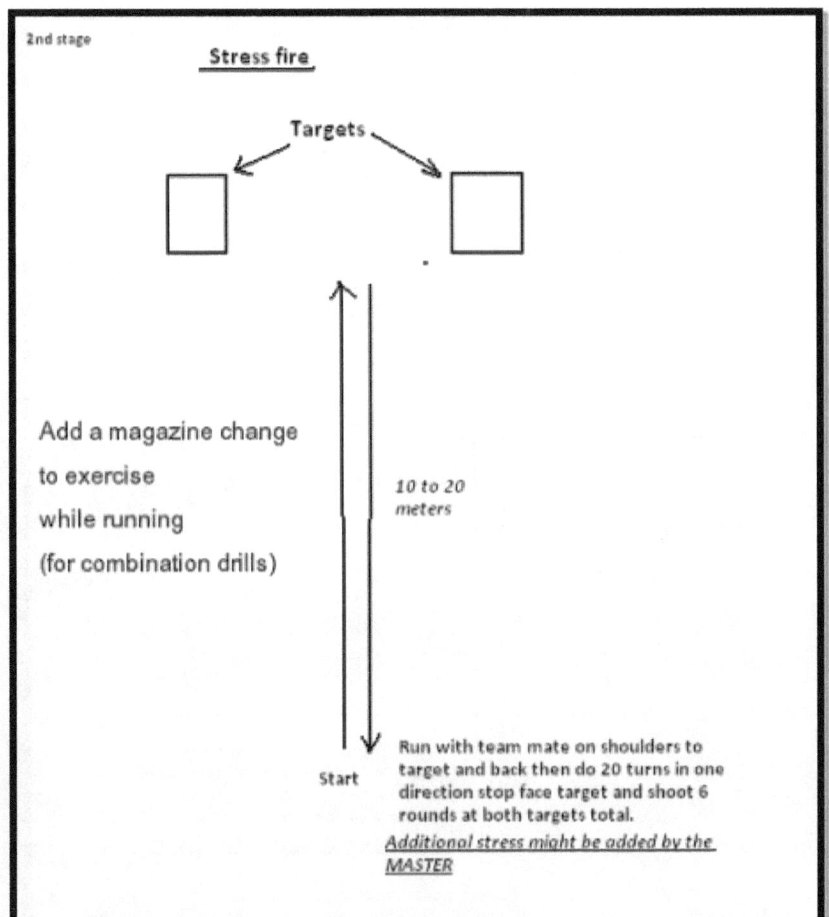
2nd stage
Stress fire
Targets
Add a magazine change
to exercise
while running
(for combination drills)
10 to 20
meters
Start
Run with team mate on shoulders to target and back then do 20 turns in one direction stop face target and shoot 6 rounds at both targets total.
Additional stress might be added by the MASTER

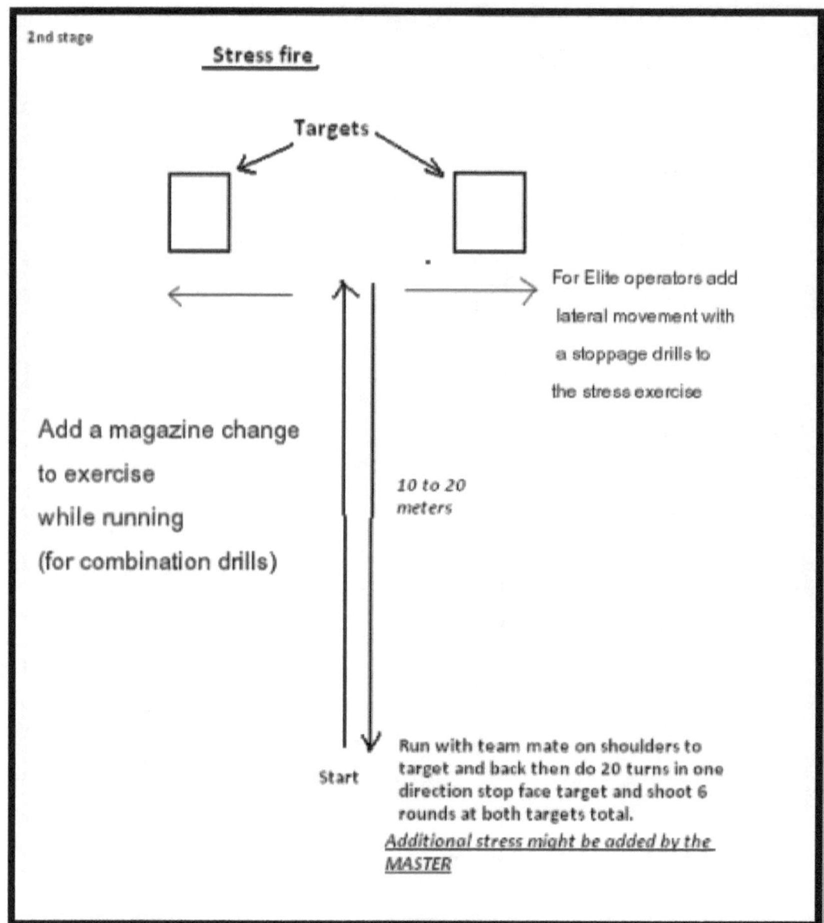
2nd stage
Stress fire
Targets
For Elite operators add
lateral movement with
a stoppage drills to
the stress exercise
Add a magazine change
to exercise
while running
(for combination drills)
10 to 20
meters
Start
Run with team mate on shoulders to
target and back then do 20 turns in one
direction stop face target and shoot 6
rounds at both targets total.
Additional stress might be added by the
MASTER

Transitioning From Rifle to Pistol

This is the ability to go from SMG/combat rifle to pistol smoothly and engage the target effectively.

Use in combination with all other drills. By this I mean when doing a stoppage drill you can also do a transition drill, or when doing magazine changes, you can also do a transition from rifle to pistol drill.

- The transition drill is applied when you have a stoppage or run out of rifle ammo and need to go to your secondary weapon.
- When you run out of ammo and the enemy is too close to do a magazine change.
- It can also be used to cover 2 angles at once; obviously, it won't be as accurate but can serve as covering fire when needed.

One way to transition is to pull the rifle to the left (if shooting right-handed) and draw the pistol one handed with your right hand and engage, this is a temporary position, as you can't change magazines from this position.

The other way to transition is to use your right hand to swing the rifle behind you so you can use your pistol with both hands and do magazine changes.

The best tactic is where you can use the rifle and the pistol without taking your firing hand off the pistol grip of the rifle, but can still access and use the pistol. Therefore, you can either use both or holster the pistol and engage with the rifle very quickly. This only works if you learn to carry the pistol on the support hand side (left side for a right-handed shooter).

Exercise Drills

Transition drill 1

This exercise will be relevant if you are in a small team or find yourself on your own in a SHTF situation where speed and proficiency is very important. Drawing with a smooth and accurate proficiency is the goal.

1. Student stands in the open
2. Place 2 targets at 10 meters
3. Engage each target with 1 round on the target from SMG/rifle
4. Do drill above, and then push the rifle to left in front of you so it hangs slightly to side but still in front
5. Do this drill above as stated above, and in addition you swing rifle completely behind you
6. Do this drill above, draw pistol with support hand while holding the rifle pistol grip with firing hand so you can if needed use the rifle immediately while manipulating the pistol (see picture below)
7. Then proceed to engage with the pistol, 1 round at each target.

REPEAT 5-10 TIMES depending on time and the type of training course the student is doing. Transition drills are not as important as aiming, stoppage drills and magazine changes and therefore don't need as much training for efficiency. The pistol is trained individually so it should be at a high level by this time. For this to work in combat you will need to turn the body so it is side on to help control recoil. See picture below for recoil control when shooting single handed:

Transition drill 2

1. Student stand in the open
2. Place 2 targets, one at 10 meters, one at 20 m
3. Put 3 rounds in SMG/rifle magazine
4. Person shoots 1 round per target, that's a total of 2 rounds for the rifle
5. When they run empty transition to pistol and engage each target 1 round per target, that's 2 rounds for the pistol.

REPEAT 5-10 TIMES

For <u>variation</u> to the transition drill (from rifle to pistol or pistol to rifle) do the drills below with the transition drill to make it more comprehensive.

1. **Without cover**: the drill can be done standing as normal, just for the accuracy and transition moving from rifle to pistol
2. **With cover**: the transition can be done behind cover and used to cover two angles in an emergency, otherwise just focus on the transition and focus on accuracy
3. **With movement**: move while doing the transition, this is difficult for accuracy and can be used to get to cover, as in covering fire.

Basic camouflage with regards to fighting rifle

The Science of Camouflage

Effective camouflage is not just common sense. Proper design and development require knowledge of how the eye and brain work.

Dealing with a target involves two steps: detecting a target and recognizing the target. Two parallel visual systems deal with detection and recognition; we can call these the focal and the ambient. Understanding how these processes work is essential to understanding camouflage.

The ambient (how the eye relates to the surroundings with regards to colors and context) system is an ancient way of seeing when you were created 6 thousand years ago, one that God gave you. This is to orientate you to surroundings before the focal (main focused vision for clear picture) system kicks in. It has been described as the **'where is it?'** system, and has a distinct anatomical basis (relating to bodily structure or pathway; the tectopulvinar). It draws most of its information from the area around the center of vision, and is critical to detection. You could see it as wider view (peripheral view). The peripheral view is important to detect movement; and peripheral vision is also used in close combat in self-defense. The reason for having a pattern that breaks up the person with light base (background) color and darker contrast is to disrupt the observer's ability to perceive structures like the shape of a human arm. This can be achieved even with basic brown stripes. How this works is the person's eye perceives the light color as the space between bushes/trees leaves (so your brain assumes that this is clear space).

The focal '**what is it?**' system is clustered near the center of vision. The nerve signal travels down the optic nerve to the Occipital lobe. Once something has been detected by the ambient system, the eye uses the focal system to try and recognize the object. The eyes see but the brain interprets, that is why a trained person's brain interprets better than a person with less understanding and training. It is therefore possible to train a person in detection techniques when looking at terrain (looking for anomalies) and the brain learns how to recognize camouflaged individuals. The brain looks at color variation, movement, and shape that doesn't fit the environment or context, combined with knowledge of what the shape of the human form is even when obscured by either brush or camouflage, of course this has its limitations as when wearing a full Ghillie suit it's almost impossible to detect the operator (if they don't move). This is of course unless the sniper/operator moves, or makes a tactical error and places them in an area where the Ghillie camouflage doesn't match the terrain e.g. lying with a grass-colored scrim in a patch of bright green grass. See examples below. This is once again the reason to watch your terrain or make sure the general terrain suits your base color. You can use large patterns to break up your outline as seen in picture below this one:

Example showing obvious camouflages failure due to inappropriate colors in the given context, using camouflage used for dry terrain and using it in a light green environment.

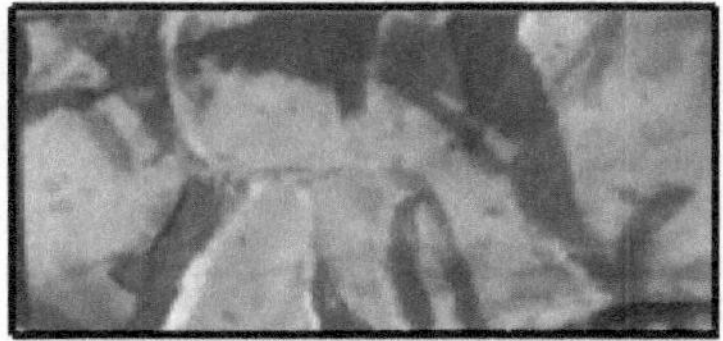

Examples showing dark lines to break up shapes:

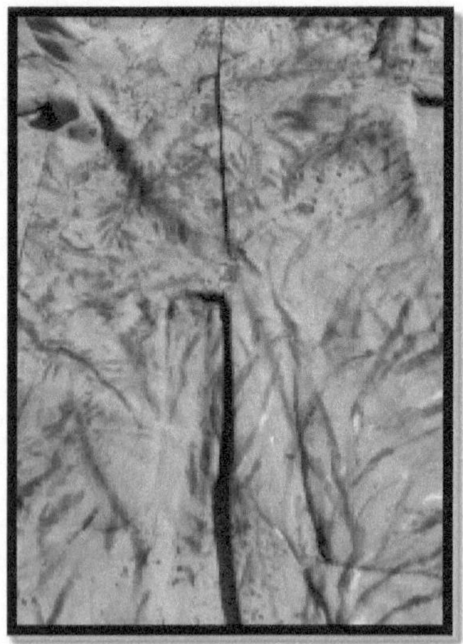

Macro and micro patterns

Two camouflage strategies are necessary, one for the ambient process (Macro pattern) and one for the focal process (Micro pattern). Leading camouflage designers base their research and practice on micro and macro patterns. Bigger patterns on top of the base tone tend to break up a person's outline better.

To make the macro and *micro pattern effective you also need to include contrast which means the colors that you use should be bright enough to contrast with the background.* If light colors are used then it would be appropriate in a context where the main colors are predominating such as in a desert where the ground colors tend to be the predominant colors (as vegetation can be very sparse).

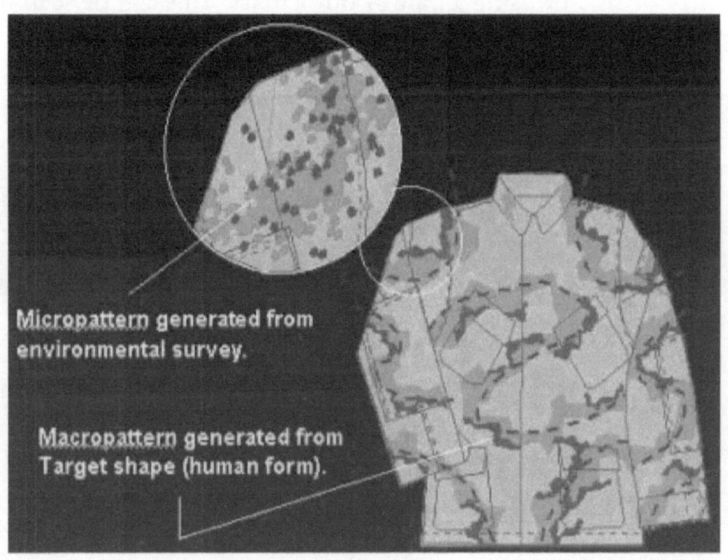

Macro features interfere with object location, micro features with identification.

The only effective way to break up the human form is well placed 'scrim' (tassel-like bits of material) that doesn't interfere with the operator's movement or weapon handling but still allows for breaking up of the human outline. It doesn't need to be elaborate or too specific in color unless used mostly in an environment where the operator will do a lot of upright walking or in a prone position where the operator will be lying down amongst grass e.g., in a reconnaissance role doing some sort of observation of a target.

The scrim doesn't have to be placed all over the arms and legs covering every inch, just on the areas that need to break down the shape of the limbs. With regard to the scrim on the arms, you need to only place it on the lower three-quarter part of the arm. It doesn't have to be on the circumference of the arm either but only along the outer edge to drop down when the arms are placed out in front the body as in the shooting of a pistol or rifle or using a pair of binoculars. This can be seen in the picture below:

Digital photo analysis

Using a product like Photoshop, one can quickly see the color palette distribution for a given scene. In the Figure below, we see the color palette alongside a photo showing hunting camouflage from Natural Gear. Just using your naked eye is probably the best way to match the main colors in your specific area of operations. This is because you would be using the camouflage in the designated terrain and can choose the natural colors that seem to mostly fit the terrain which is seen by your eye. This is the most natural and accurate way.

The color palette analysis from a digital photo provides a useful display of color tones in a scene. Additional analysis could be done to e.g., determine the most frequent pixel color. Note how the man's unnatural horizontal lines happen to coincide with the horizontal logs. Horizontal lines tend to give away game and humans so it would be good to hide among natural horizontal lines like low hanging branches.

Example of a horizontal pattern below (South African pattern):

Where horizontal lines need to be broken up you can also use scrim of different lengths; the environment will dictate the color of the scrim. Keeping the scrim similar in size and color to the surrounding is important to blend in.

grass colored sc

Base tone

It's important that the base tone be one commonly found in the terrain of application. For example, a Natural Gear product is shown in this next figure using a photographically derived base tone.

An example of a photographically derived base tone in camouflage from Natural Gear

Black features

Black is very rare in nature as a natural color, especially in desert settings. Instead, the eye will see black shapes in a camouflage pattern as 'depth'. If you switch black for grey, you'll lose the sense of depth with a pattern. At close range, you'll see little black in nature. At longer ranges e.g., 100 meters, deeper shades and shadows tend towards black in color. If you use color palette analysis from digital photos, you can see how the frequency distribution for various shades will change with a target viewed against a background at various ranges.

Therefore, guidelines are generally to use brown instead of black when designing desert patterns. Small amounts of black can be used for urban applications. The more trees there are in the terrain, the more you could incorporate black into the pattern for the edges to break sharp lines. Trees tend to have a grey whitish bark in African plains and most parts of the world, so incorporate some grey.

It's a better idea to use small amounts of black, if, any to break lines of the edges of the garment where needed and as stated above certain desert environments will need *no black* in the pattern but some scrim will help to break the outline of the operator's uniform (arms and legs). Use dark brown to break up the outlines instead of black when in a desert. This could be using a tiger stripe or just using large area coloring as your macro pattern, for example coloring one arm mostly light brown and the one leg mostly ochre or oxide.

The pattern shown below is about 95-98 percent mix of olive green, light brown and beige as the backdrop color which is good for sandy areas because sand has a light grey color to an orange color in areas with a lot of iron.

Vertical lines

Gravity effects result in most vegetation growing vertically. Hunters are trained to spot game by looking for horizontal lines. Some camouflage patterns have vertical features but these can then be lost in overlaid patterns of sticks and leaves. It would behoove you to consider where you will be using your camouflage and in what position your body will be in when considering the patterns on your outfit or overall, as the position of your body should dictate the position of the lines even if they are light in color and not definite such as a black or dark brown color.

Any parallel horizontal lines on the leg will show up as vertical lines when lying prone. Black lines on the picture below indicate the vertical lines and their direction when in a prone position. Keep in mind that the pattern will have to fit into the overall pattern and scheme of the camouflage pattern to blend nicely when standing upright as well. This is achieved by painting a shrub or small tree that allows for the vertical lines in a prone position to mimic either upright branches (as seen by the greyish white line) or in some cases grass (as in ochre lines) and an appropriate pattern in the vertical position.

This next picture shows the front and side of the leg of a camouflage garment:

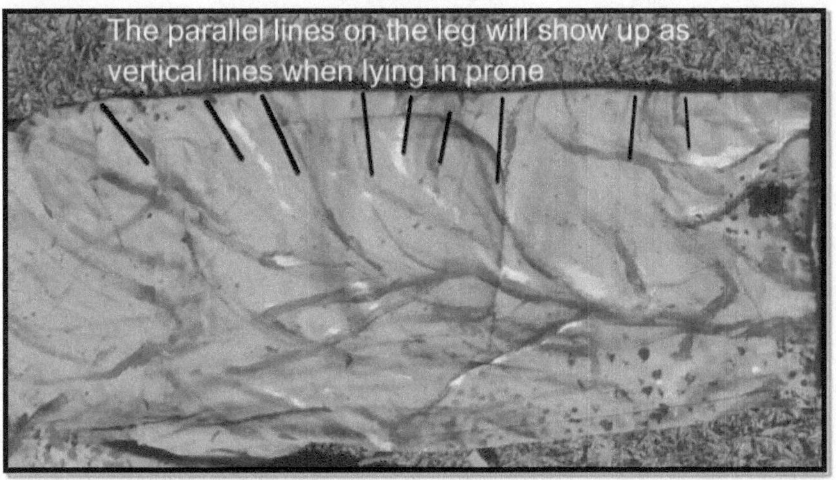

The back of the same garment with a slightly different pattern for a better overall blending into the environment when in prone position:

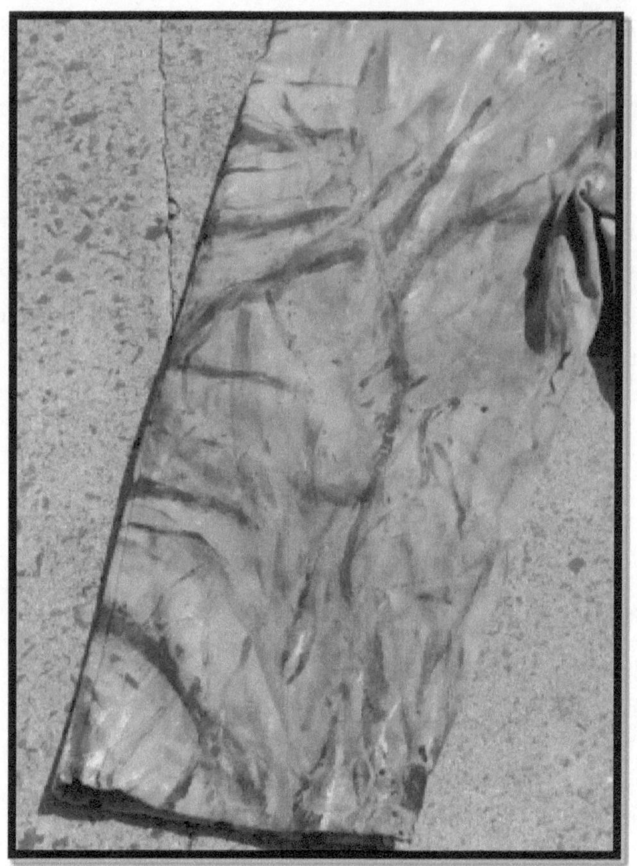

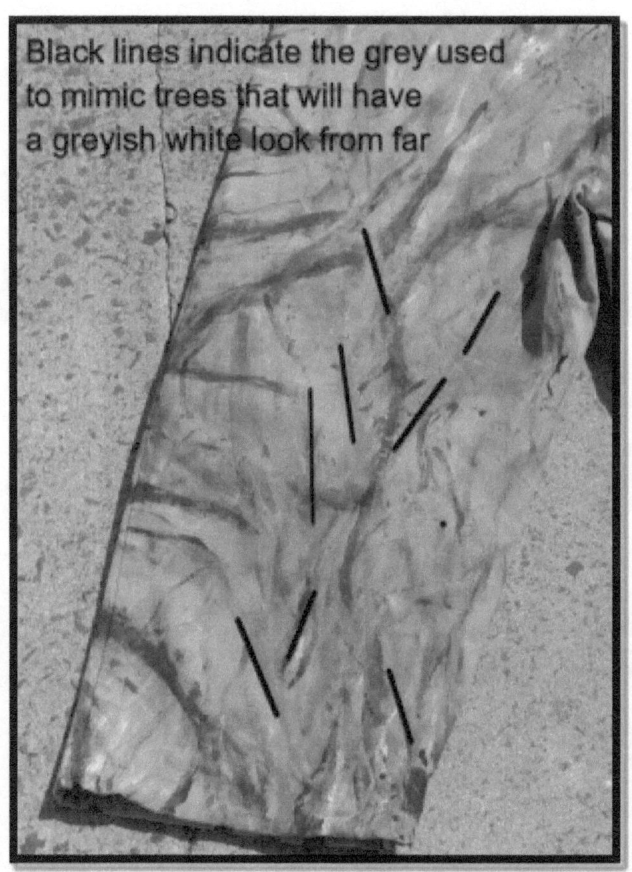
Black lines indicate the grey used
to mimic trees that will have
a greyish white look from far

The overall camouflage pattern in a realistic environment:

Shadows

Let shadow patterns occur naturally. Don't try and model shadow in the design because if the natural light is not throwing shadows e.g., it's overcast, the pattern will fail. The human eye is very good at picking out bad lighting effects, which is often observed in computer graphic renderings and when manipulating digital photographs.

Dark colors, especially black, have featured strongly in jungle camouflage patterns. There the vegetation will produce a lot of dark areas under the tree canopy, so you're less likely to be caught out in the open where no vegetation could be casting shadows on you. The 'tiger stripe' effect used in jungle patterns works because there is a dark green/black background. An observer sees 'through' the dark parts of the pattern because they blend with the background, and this breaks up shapes better. This is illustrated clearly in the figure below.

Tiger stripes don't have to be black. In fact, as long as the color scheme is evenly weighted such that you can't really tell if its light stripes on a dark background or vice versa, then the stripes break up shapes against both dark and light backgrounds (of basically the same color). This figure shows a modern woodland tiger stripe pattern using digital edge effects:

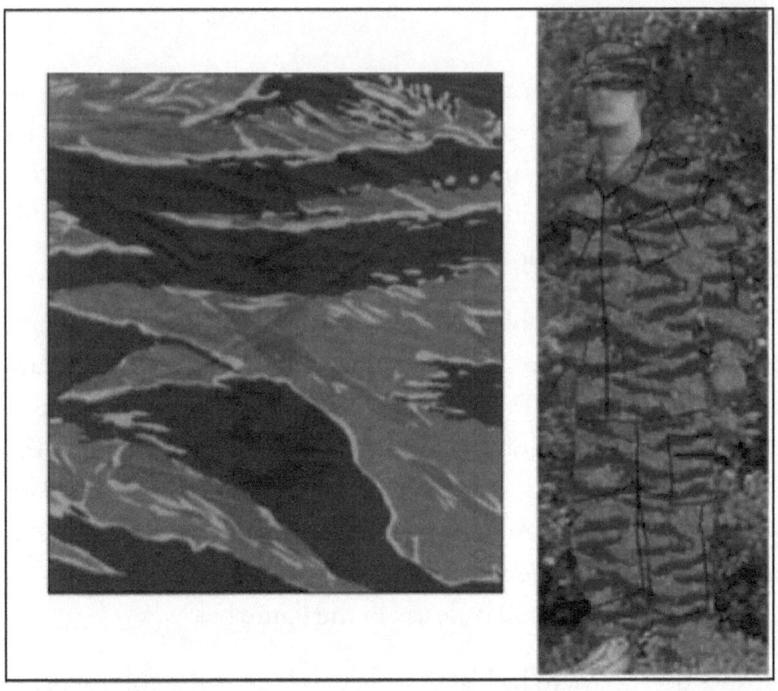

In this picture, you can see that the dark olive green of the backpack blends well with the shadows made by the bush:

The following pictures demonstrate some uniforms that will work well in the shade as they are dark in color:

The first two pictures above show the tiger stripe effect. The eye sees the dark part of the pattern as part of the background. The stripes therefore require a lot of dark regions in the terrain, which one would expect to find under the tree canopy of forest and jungle but not in many other locations.

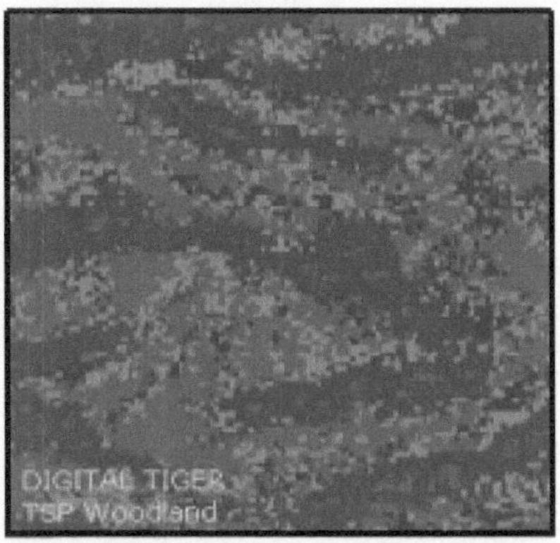

The above pattern is a digital woodland tiger stripe pattern. Note how the stripes don't have to be black, and that they will work against backgrounds of either color.

Edges

If the pattern has strong edges to its colored regions, it's easier for an observer to focus on you and begin the process of shape recognition. Patterns that interfere with focus make identification of that object difficult. For this reason, modern camouflage designs are using soft edges e.g., 'digital' camouflage. The edges of collared regions of the design are blurry to the eye. If the pattern of dark and light are dispersed enough you might not have shape recognition, especially if the light-colored aspects of the pattern are large enough to hide the separate arms and legs by making one of them light and the other darker as part of the larger macro pattern.

The same effect can be achieved by using small spots/dots in a wedge, making a dark area (gives an effect where dark areas appear as shadow) in certain areas of the camouflage pattern. This is time consuming to make but worth the effort if it's for an outfit you will use for recon purposes. Strong brown colors on the edges can also give you the disruptive properties, two patterns that will work well in this regard are shown below. The picture below could use more definition in the pattern e.g. **contrast** would be more successful because this creates contrast that breaks up the outline.

The picture above shows the Russian Spetsnaz pattern superimposed over African terrain – it's not necessarily the terrain that this camouflage was meant for but is used for illustration purposes. This is a fairly good match of camouflage material to terrain, and the pattern will work fairly well.

Range effects

Pattern blob size

Bigger pattern features will hold up better at longer range, whereas smaller micro features will fade into the base tone. The US Marine Corps researched various patterns and optimized the colors for their environment. Field tests indicated that CADPAT (Canadian

Disruptive Pattern) is the best short to medium range camouflage (10 - 150m); Rhodesian is the best medium to long range camouflage (50 to 500m), and an enlarged sparse Tiger stripe camouflage 3rd (50 to 250m). They then copied the CADPAT and enlarged the pattern by 45% resulting in MARPAT (the Marine Pattern).

Canadian CAPPAT pattern:

Rhodesian camouflage (keep in mind that the darker camouflaged material on the left will work better):

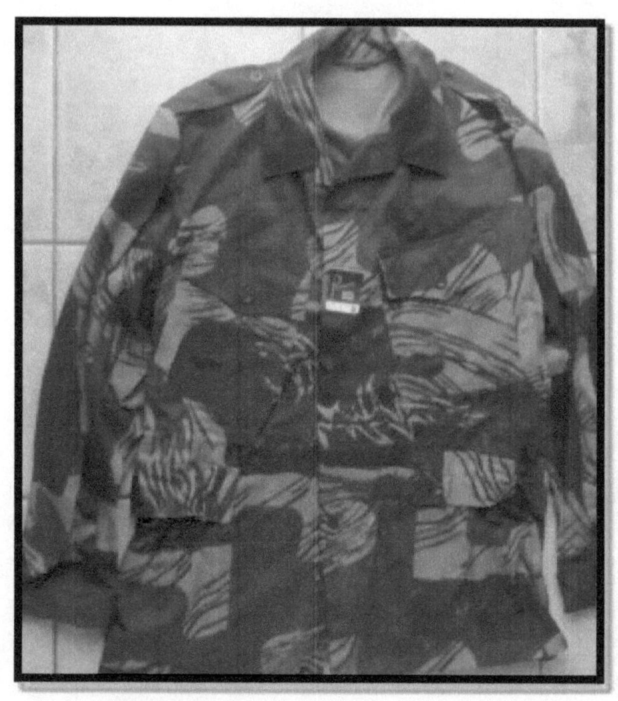

Pattern clutter

If a pattern is too cluttered, the wearer looks very dark when viewed at a distance. A lot of 'stick and leaf' patterns can look good close up, but perform poorly when viewed at a distance. The solution to long range merging is to use a pattern that is more 'open' i.e., has more base tone with fewer overlaid patterns. This next picture shows merging effects on two people:

The long-range merging effect arises from a cluttered camouflage pattern. Viewed at a distance, the pattern deteriorates into a dark blob.

Pattern artwork

Critics of popular hunting camouflage patterns refer to such patterns as 'sticks and leaves artwork'. This works very well at close range but the artwork detail is lost at longer range. Many also seem to be quite cluttered. Hunters aren't being observed from long range by deer through binoculars/similar, so a hunting pattern can be optimized for closer ranges compared with military applications.

Some patterns used by hunters can also be used as a **base pattern** to make you really good camouflage, especially if the camouflage is a good basic pattern with few colors such as beige and brown. To this you can then add colors that will suit your terrain and use the base pattern of the original camouflage to be the large pattern and add some small features to this for a macro and micro pattern combination. If you use both light and dark brown, grey (dark and almost white), and red (ochre) with a base of an orange / rusty color you should be able to make a good desert camouflage.

Design simplicity

The more complex a camouflage pattern, the more situation-specific it becomes. A lot of stick-and-leaf patterns can perform poorly in very grassy regions, for example.

This is important in terrain that has a mostly homogenous color scheme such as deserts where 90% of the surrounding color is a rusty orange color because of the iron content in the soil, that is intermittently scattered with bushes that will be dark (olive) green, but will probably still have areas where the rocks will be a whitish grey color. Therefore, a little white and grey will help with mostly a base color of light orange then add some brown for areas with bushes. Having a bit of each color will help to blend you into the environment and makes for a good long-range pattern as there are no large dark areas indicating arms and legs.

Don't miss out!

Visit the website below and you can sign up to receive emails whenever Mike Harland publishes a new book. There's no charge and no obligation.

https://books2read.com/r/B-A-BCLG-EPMTB

BOOKS 2 READ

Connecting independent readers to independent writers.